The Alternative
STAG

Also available from Virgin Books:
The Alternative Hen

The Alternative
STAG

Genna Hayman & Kirstie Rowson

First published in Great Britain in 2003 by
Virgin Books Ltd
Thames Wharf Studios · Rainville Road · London W6 9HA
Copyright © Genna Hayman & Kirstie Rowson 2003

**Great care has been taken with this guide to be as accurate and up-to-date as
possible, but details such as addresses, telephone numbers, website and email
addresses are liable to change. The publishers and authors cannot accept
responsibility for any consequences arising from the use of this book. We
would be delighted to receive any corrections and suggestions for inclusion in
the next edition.**

ISBN 0 7535 0801 X

Designed and typeset by Lovelock & Co.
Printed and bound in Great Britain by Mackays of Chatham

Contents

Acknowledgements

We would like to thank Elliot Clark for his insight and witticisms, David Hayman, Alex di Silvestro, Anand Shukla, Dan Edgerton, Adrian Kennedy, Seb Grant and Kim Porter for all helping us to make this book a reality.

The Alternative Stag

First thoughts of a stag do inevitably involve beer and strippers. But if you're looking for greater inspiration for the lucky man's final night of freedom with the lads, then read on …

You know the score: beer, beer, strippers, more beer and definitely one comatose stag completely oblivious to the banana and cream antics on show before his blurry eyes. Or even his role as a stage prop as he dribbles away, while maintaining a loving clutch on his trusty pint. All undeniably great fun but if you are only let off the leash every once in a while, you'll be looking for something a bit different to make the most of the weekend.

On the other hand, you might have a stag that just isn't into that kind of thing. Allegedly, they do exist.

Either way, *The Alternative Stag* will give you loads of great ideas to get you started on organising a stag night worthy of becoming the stuff of urban legend, without breaking up the happy couple.

Getting Organised

Organised? We're not talking diary notes and gilt-edged invites but organisation is the key to a memorable event. This is not a time to rely on spontaneity to do your mate proud – there is nothing worse for a stag party than an uninspired night, spending half the time traipsing around a city you don't know, without any idea of where to go. If you're thinking of winging it, rest assured, you've got more chance of fondling Kylie's rear bumper than going down in history as the man responsible for a stag do to remember.

For those of you best men who think you haven't got a hope in hell of getting it together, this handbook will show you how easy it is. And it can all be arranged via email at work, providing your boss's back is turned.

There's advice on scoping out dates and locations, who to invite, themes, an Alternative Stag speech, drinking games, activities, international events and sporting fixtures, overseas options, and a to do checklist. The Alternative Directory also provides a contacts list to help you get started with looking for activities and accommodation for a range of UK destinations.

Stags on Tour – Scoping Out Dates and Locations

It goes without saying that you will have a range of lads on the weekend and so budgets and availability will have to be considered. But a night out in the stag's hometown is, quite frankly, not an option. Not only because this should be a night out with a difference rather than just a night out at the local, but also because bumping into a neighbour, relative or friend of the bride-to-be at any point is hardly conducive to giving your mate enough space to let his hair or trousers down.

Britain is full of great cities, or you might want to jump on a cheapo flight if budget allows. Wherever you go, it is worth checking out the Directory, Events, Sporting Fixtures and Over the Water Getaways sections in this book to see what's what.

Most importantly, even if you're not the most organised of men you need to get a date in all the lads', or in this instance bucks', diaries as early as possible. Avoid the nightmare of trying to co-ordinate a dozen lads by booking them up before it becomes an issue. Remember that although they might not be 'that kind of bloke', if they've got a bird, it is highly probable that she's got their weekends planned for the next decade.

Traditionally the bride and groom send out their official invitations six to eight weeks in advance of the wedding, so aim to do at least the same thing for the stag do. Allow more time if possible so that you are guaranteed to be able to get accommodation for a large group. And, of course, being as brides, mothers and mothers-in-law tend to get the hump about husbands-to-be showing up bruised or useless a week before the wedding, plan to have the stag do at least two weeks before the big day. Or his and your lives won't be worth living.

Highlights to think about

◆ Range of budgets and availability.
◆ Home or away.
◆ A date for the diaries.
◆ Your place in the wedding schedule.

Invitations

Who to invite, who not to invite? It's a toss up. Is it better to have the future father-in-law not speaking to the stag because he's hacked off he wasn't invited? Or to have the possibility of him threatening your mate's wedding tackle after witnessing his drunken mauling of the saucy stripper? And do you want the world and his wide boys there, or would you prefer to keep it to a select few? If you've got a tricky situation and are not sure which way to go, the answer is simple – why not have two stag nights? An Alternative Stag do with your real mates and a second stag night down the pub with the outlaws (soon to be in-laws) and wide boys. Nightmare scenario neatly sidestepped. No casualties.

Invitations can be straightforward. But if you've already decided what type of do you'll be having and the dates are informally agreed, you might want to really go to town with them. They are an excellent excuse to get into character for your theme and roll out a couple of embarrassing photos of or quotes from the stag. Just bear in mind that the more effort you make in organising the stag do, the more effort the bucks will be willing to put into the actual event.

Themes

Bad luck. This isn't just about embarrassing the stag when it's too late for him to do anything about it. It's about all of you. But before you burn this book, consider the following:

◆ With a load of you all making an arse of yourselves, you'll have a right laugh that'll give you something to talk about for years to come.

◆ You'll get some great original material for the wedding speech you've been dreading since the moment the stag asked you to be his best man.

◆ Women the world over are inexplicably attracted to spending time with any men who exude confidence and are up for fun, so that should give your stag plenty of opportunities for some harmless flirting while he's away.

◆ They will also consider an ugly bloke if he makes them laugh.

Strange but true. It's the understated balancer; money and a great car versus a washboard stomach and demigod looks, versus a sense of humour. You could look like Bernard Manning and still pull if you can make them laugh. Although, in his case, he'd need a pretty chunky wad of cash to get them slaughtered first. Praise be.

Clearly, pulling opportunities are (for the benefit of any girlfriends or wives reading this book) purely for the single lads in the party. But, as a great mate of the stag, it's also your duty to give him a send-off to remember and reminisce over in future years, when all he's got to look forward to are nights in front of the TV with the missus and dirty nappies.

Failing that, just treat it as an experiment.

A few words to the wise

First, it is worth keeping the theme a secret from the stag until the last minute to add to the impact. You'll be glad you did when you see the mixed look of horror and amusement on his face.

Second, if you're going overseas, it's always a good idea to pick a theme that'll appeal to the locals. A classic would be a stag party setting off for Sweden all dressed as Björn Borg in his whites – wooden tennis racket an essential. Naturally, it would be unfair to deny the stag his moment of glory, and so a blond wig for him gives you the choice of taking Martina Navratilova or a butch Anna Kournikova along with you too.

And, third, included are some ideas for challenges for the stag on the main night if you're up to it. It's probably worth being pretty hammered before you even think about handing them out. A horrendously impaired sense of judgement after an initial drinking warm-up tends to help things along ...

James Bond

Shaken not schtirred, my dear. This is the opportunity to work those innuendos to the max.

Outfit

◆ Easy. DJ or tuxedo – get all the bucks to go dressed in the same attire, with the stag in the other option to differentiate him, or even as Bond in his diving gear.

◆ If you've got a game-on group of bucks, complement your *Schtag*-Bond to his finest by all dressing up as evil geniuses, or even show a bit of leg as Bond girls …

Props

◆ Water pistols.

◆ Any portable gadget you can lay your hands on.

◆ White pussies to stroke throughout the night.

Something for the stag

◆ Own martini glass.

◆ Fluffy handcuffs to arrest those feisty female villains.

◆ Concealed weapon.

Challenges

◆ Persuade a vixen to buy you a dry martini, shaken not stirred.

◆ Re-enact the opening credits of Bond and convince two girls to be your silhouetted dancers, while your bucks recreate the track 'Nobody Does It Better'.

◆ Name ten Bond girls or drink a tequila shot.

◆ Go undercover and get a girl to draw a third nipple on you so you can pose as Scaramanga [*The Man With The Golden Gun*].

◆ Arrest a female suspect, handcuff yourself to her and challenge her to a drinking contest. You must down a pint, she must down a half, both using your cuffed hand only. The winner keeps the handcuffs.

◆ Deliver these Bond winning one-liners throughout the night:

– I think your mouth is exactly the right size … for me, that is [*From Russia With Love*].

– Well, that's quite a nice little nothing you are almost wearing; I approve [*Diamonds Are Forever*].

– How clumsy of me, now I've gotten you all wet! But my Martini is still dry [*Never Say Never Again*].

Activities

Check out the activity ideas and Alternative Directory for:

◆ Horse racing or Polo.

◆ Clay pigeon shooting.

Go Roman

Back when women were second-class citizens and men were men ... even though they wore sandals and skirts.

Outfit

◆ A couple of options here, depending on how much effort you want to make. Take your pick from gladiators, Caesar or Roman servants, but make sure your stag stands out from the bucks.

◆ Sheets for togas.

◆ Sandals.

◆ Gladiator outfits (realistically, lads, you've got to hire these costumes – your granny's pleated skirt just won't do).

Props

◆ Sword and shield for the gladiators.

Something for the stag

◆ Laurel wreath for a Caesar stag's head.

◆ Short curly wig for the stamp of Caesar's true authority.

◆ Sword and shield if he's the only gladiator.

Challenges

◆ Demand that a serving wench brings a full goblet of wine to your table. Keep going until either someone actually gets it for you, or you get tired of being repeatedly slapped across the face.

◆ Rack up your sex appeal by getting a buxom wench to draw some chest hair on you with her eyeliner.

◆ Name ten films featuring Romans for a reward of your bucks' choice.

◆ Organise your bucks to join you in a chariot race to the next bar (if you don't have horses and chariots then you'll have to make do with piggybacks). The losers buy the next round.

◆ Order one of your bucks to be your point man – he must convince a nubile goddess to come and administer your drink to you in a manner of her choosing.

◆ Deliver these winning one-liners throughout the night:

– Friends, Romans, countrymen … (when you're ordering a round at the bar) [*Julius Caesar*, Shakespeare].

– At my signal, unleash hell! (use this as a signal to all down your drinks) [*Gladiator*].

Activities

Check out the activity ideas and Alternative Directory for:

◆ Wine tasting and vineyards.

◆ Chariot racing, aka a motor experience.

Cowboys

Strong, blunt and rugged. And good for making an arse of yourselves, especially if you know the words to Oklahoma. A winner.

Outfit

◆ Stetson, or any old cowboy hat.

◆ Plaid shirt and neckerchief.

◆ Jeans (but check with venues for dress codes in advance).

Props

◆ Water pistol.

◆ Pack of cards.

Something for the stag

◆ Sheriff's badge.

◆ Cigar.

◆ Lasso and spurs.

Challenges

◆ Find two cowgirls to show you how to do a hoedown.

- Single out a foxy cowgirl in the saloon. Challenge her to a shot duel. Line up a couple of shots and see who can down them fastest.

- Lasso a feisty filly and release her once she's bought you a stiff drink.

- Name ten cowboy actors in order to receive a reward of your bucks' choice.

- It's time to show your riding skills to the bar. Mount your steed (or a chair) and show a female volunteer your best lap dance moves. Encourage her to follow your example.

- Organise your cowboys for a race to the next bar (unless you've got your steed tethered outside the saloon, you'll have to make do with piggybacks). The losers buy the next round.

- Deliver these winning one-liners throughout the night to get into character:

- Don't squat with your spurs on.

- What's a mighty fine lady like you doing in a bar like this?

- Why, you yellow-bellied, lily-livered rascal.

- Howdy, ma'am, let me show ya how to take the bull by the horns.

Activities

Check out the activity ideas and Alternative Directory for:

- Horse racing fixtures.

Vikings

You might have problems justifying raping and pillaging in the twenty-first century, so concentrate on the boorish oaf aspect and you'll go far.

Outfit

◆ Think hairy. Think horny helmets. Think *skol, skol, skol*.

◆ Brown loo mat for your shoulders (preferably new, or at least not stained).

◆ Sacking tunics, rope belts and material straps round your calves.

Props

◆ Swords and shields.

◆ Hip flasks.

Something for the stag

◆ Back combed hair or bird's nest wig a must.

◆ Fake facial hair if he's not already a beardy bloke.

Challenges

◆ After a fine jug of hearty English ale, challenge one of your fellow revellers to a belching contest. Loudest wins a pint.

◆ Demand a buxom serving wench brings you a drink from the bar to wherever you're sat, without leaving your chair. Carry on until you get a drink or verbal abuse.

◆ Show these Anglo-wenches what a real man is made of – give one of them a Viking lap dance. Alternatively, your point man must convince one of the wenches to give you a lap dance. The bucks decide.

◆ Challenge one of your fellow Vikings to a wife-carrying contest. Choose your finish line and find two willing village maidens to partake in the frivolities.

Extras

◆ See the 'Stags' heading under the Drinking Games chapter and adapt it to 'Vikings'. The only differences are that the Viking in the spotlight uses cupped hands to demonstrate horns on a helmet, and the bucks either side use both hands to air paddle the Viking ship the three of them are on. If either of the bucks paddles 'in the boat', they are penalised.

Activities

Check out the activity ideas and Alternative Directory for:

◆ Viking Festivals.

◆ A trip to Scandinavia.

Circus Performers

Roll up, roll up. And roll home a few hours later. It's time to amaze the crowds with your ... er ... acts.

Outfit

◆ Take your pick. With the best man as the ringmaster, what could go wrong? The rest of the bucks can choose from clowns, tightrope walkers, ballerinas, lion tamers, human cannonballs, acrobats, circus freaks, mimes or circus animals.

Props

◆ Silly string and balloons for clowns, and anything else that suits your individual characters.

◆ A bag of candyfloss never goes amiss with the ladies.

◆ A toffee apple (for one of the challenges).

Something for the stag

◆ It can only be the Strongman. With a leopard-skin print leotard (or vest and shorts for the self-conscious stag), handlebar moustache, black bovver boy boots, dumb-bells and slicked back hair, he'll look a real treat.

Best man duties

◆ As the ringmaster, you're going to have an added role – you're running the show! Make the most of winning one-liners such as 'Roll up, roll up for the greatest show on earth,' and 'Be amazed at the death-defying feats of the world's strongest stag.' This is one of the themes requiring the most effort to make it work. So yes, you too are going to have to put yourself on the line to make this a night to remember for your stag.

Challenges

◆ Although the Strongman is indeed strong, he is also (dis)graceful. Wow the crowds with a split leap and a somersault across the bar without giving yourself groin strain.

◆ Demonstrate your strength while the ringmaster drums up an audience with his banter.

◆ Ask female onlookers to mark your biceps out of ten. Once you receive a ten (or a four if you're Mr Puniverse), the bucks have to buy you a drink of your choice.

◆ Entertain the ladies with a 'World's Strongest Stag' lap dance, provided they're willing to reward you with a drink. Alternatively, convince a glamorous showgirl to give you a lap dance.

◆ Say to a lady of your bucks' choice, 'Would you like to feel my bell ends?' (dumb-bells advisable for this one).

♦ Find a beautiful magician's assistant to help you make a toffee apple disappear in one minute. She can feed it to you how she likes.

Activities

Check out the activity ideas and Alternative Directory for:

♦ Circus school.

Star Wars

Classic. Weapons, fit birds, action and adventure. May the force be with you.

Outfit

◆ Again, it's best if the stag stands out, so all the bucks going as Jedi knights with the stag as Princess Leia, or all as storm troopers with the stag as Darth Vader, would be the favourites. Or, alternatively, go completely to town and go for the full cast list. (Wouldn't recommend anyone going as Ja-Ja Binks, as you might find you have to put an end to the irritating alien git before the end of the night.)

Props

◆ Water pistol (just for those of you out there who are loose cannons – not metallic pistols or you'll be liable to get shot by the real authorities).

◆ Walkie-talkies.

◆ Green light-sabres if the bucks are all Jedis.

Something for the stag

◆ Red light-sabre if he's Darth Vader.

- Well, Leia outfits are the stuff of contemporary wet dreams. A baggy sheet and Swiss schoolmistress buns on each side of the head for the shy stag. For the cocky stag, the full-on *Return of the Jedi* gold bikini number and neck chain, with woven and flowing locks.

Challenges

- You must save the Alliance from the dark forces of the Empire. Scope out the bar and convince a woman to give you one item of her clothing that you need to bribe the Emperor. You have two minutes to save the universe.
- Chat to a girl of your bucks' choice and at an inappropriate moment, lean into her and whisper, 'I can feeeeeel your presence.'
- You've seen the training Luke went through with Yoda. On your way to the bar to collect the next round, demonstrate to your bucks how athletic and acrobatic you are too.
- Name 15 *Star Wars* characters or down a tequila shot.
- You've hurt your arm in a battle. Convince a princess in the bar to feed your drink to you, however she chooses.

Activities

Check out the activity ideas and Alternative Directory for:
- Shooting ranges.
- Outdoor activity centres.

Elvis Lives

One for the money. Two for the show. Three to get ready, now go, go, go.

Outfit

◆ Bucks as Hawaiian Elvis (Hawaiian shirts, lei and dark trousers), or who-ate-all-the-pies Elvis (velour jumpsuits and jewellery).

Props

◆ Microphone.

◆ Cheeseburger and loo seat.

◆ 70s Elvis-style shades.

Something for the stag

◆ There can only be one. The white, rhinestone-encrusted, wing-collared Elvis. Las Vegas, eat your heart out.

Challenges

◆ Every time anyone gives you a drink or a compliment, reply with, 'Thanuverymuch, uh-huh.' If you forget, you have to down a two-finger fine.

- You are the King. Choose your point man, who has to go and find some adoring fans to scream at you. You must down five fingers once he achieves this.
- You're all shook up. Burst into song with 'Hound Dog' in a public place to demonstrate your knee-trembling and lip-wobbling routine. Depending on the mark out of ten your audience gives you, that's the finger fine all your bucks must down.
- It's hot under the stage lights. Cool yourself off seductively with an ice cube until you've managed to make at least five girls laugh.
- Name ten Elvis songs for a reward of your bucks' choice.

Activities

Check out the activity ideas and Alternative Directory for:
- Recording studio experience.

Austin Powers

Oh behave.

Outfit

◆ This involves a fair amount of effort. The ideal is that the stag goes as the International Man of Mystery himself, while the bucks go as Fat Bastard, Dr Evil, Gold Member, Number 2, Scott, Frau Farbissina, Vanessa Kensington, Felicity Shagwell and Foxxy Cleopatra.

◆ The other option is that everyone goes as casual Austin Powers in the same outfits, but the stag has the pièce de résistance with the blue velvet suit and white shirt with the ruched collar.

Props

◆ Thick black-rimmed glasses.

◆ Water pistols.

◆ Cold leg wax strips (for one of the challenges).

Something for the stag

◆ False teeth with the suitable amount of cheesy build-up.

◆ Chest wig.

Challenges

◆ While talking to a sexy woman (of your bucks' choice), lick or suck your finger seductively, and then trail it across the woman's clothing, growling, 'We must get you out of those wet clothes.'

◆ Vanessa's not happy with your body hair. Luckily your bucks have brought some cold wax strips. Ask a willing sexy minx to wax your calf for you.

◆ Dr Evil is up to no good. Down two shots of tequila and warm up your karate muscles with some shadow sparring between each shot. Your Shaguar awaits for you to race off to save the world. Again.

◆ You're undercover. The assailant you're tracking is dressed as a woman but has guns strapped to 'her' chest and masked as fake boobs. You have an idea who it is. Find out if you're right with some 60s bar cricket. A slap round the face gets you a six and means the bucks all have to down a shot of tequila.

◆ Find out whether you are more of an International Man of Mystery than your bucks by leading the 'I have never' drinking game with a racy first-round statement that is a lie (so you have to drink too). [See the Drinking Games section for details.]

◆ Deliver these winning one-liners throughout the night:

- I am a *sexy* beast!

- Do I make you horny?

- Oh behave …

Activities

Check out the activity ideas and Alternative Directory for:

◆ Motor experience days.

Alternatives

◆ If you know who Björn and Benny are, you might want to try an Abba theme night. A club full of Agnethas and Anni-Frids … Sigh.

◆ A 70s theme never goes amiss. A bit of a cop-out for a stag night, but better than nothing at all. The only way you can begin to justify it is by going all out as 70s porn stars.

Convicts

You don't get out much. So this is your opportunity to go for it.

Outfit

◆ Take your pick. The stripy number or the arrows. Or if you're really flash, the bright orange.

◆ Black boots.

Props

◆ Spoons for digging tunnels.

Something for the stag

◆ Ball and chain (yes, you can buy them).

◆ Make-up for a black eye (it's tough in prison).

◆ Soap on a rope.

◆ Fake tattoos, if he hasn't got any real ones already.

Challenges

◆ As an inmate you don't have any money, but you do know how to trade. Offer a woman a lap dance in return for her buying you a drink. Alternatively, your bucks will buy you a drink if you can convince her to give you a lap dance.

◆ You're going to try to escape. But you need a disguise. You have three minutes to get as many items of clothing from women as you can. Every item is a two-finger drinking fine you can hand out to a buck.

◆ You've been on a chain gang for years. A three-legged race would be far too easy for you guys. Try a four-legged race to the next bar (that's three bodies for those of you looking for a calculator). The losers get the next round in.

◆ If you have to eat another bowl of porridge in your life, you'll be violently ill. Settle your stomach with a drink. Ask one of the lovely female day visitors to buy you a drink and administer it to you however she wants.

◆ Trade some smokes for a drink with a female warden.

Activities

Check out the activity ideas and Alternative Directory for:

◆ Outdoor activity centres, including blindfolded driving.

◆ Skid-pan motor experiences for a quick getaway.

Sporting Heroes

Easy and very effective.

Outfit

◆ Bucks, first on centre court is Mr Björn Borg. En masse.

◆ Next to serve – the stag will transform into the shapely Ms Anna Kournikova (although he'll probably look more like Martina Navratilova – hopefully). Or perhaps Serena Williams in a sporty skin-tight black catsuit, although that leaves the problem of where to keep his balls …

Props

◆ For the bucks: wooden tennis rackets, sweat bands, tight 70s-style tennis whites, and wigs a must. Go crazy and throw in a tank top for good measure.

◆ Tennis balls.

◆ Scissors (for one of the challenges).

Something for the stag

◆ Anna Kournikova – long blonde tresses in a plait, tennis skirt, tennis racket, socks with bobbles, padded sports bra or fake boobs.

- Serena Williams – braided black wig, anything skimpy and vaguely sporty that you can find, tennis racket.

Challenges

- Ask a woman if she'd give you her opinion on something – are your balls firm enough for a good game?

- Send your point man out to gather some of the female eye candy that's been distracting you on court. He must bring them back one at a time. If you manage to keep the first one entertained so that she's still talking to you by the time the second is introduced, then that's game and set. If they're both still there when the third one is introduced, it's game, set and match. Tequila shots all round.

- Whichever tennis tottie you might be, stand at the bar and show some female groupies the classic calendar shot. Hitch up the back of your tennis skirt to flash them some butt cheek while licking your finger seductively at the same time.

- As Björn and Anna, you're both into clothing ranges. You're thinking of launching a new line of women's lingerie. As part of your research you need to know what women are wearing now. You have three minutes to cut as many labels from women's lingerie as you can.

- Name fifteen Wimbledon champions to win a prize of your bucks' choice. Or face a drinking fine.

Activities

Check out the activity ideas and Alternative Directory for:

◆ Sporting event fixtures.

◆ Polo.

Alternatives

◆ Other recognisable sports celebrities include: Des Lynham, John McEnroe, Muhammad Ali, 80s-style Kevin Keegan, 1966 England football team.

◆ If you're going overseas, pick a renowned sporting hero from that country to get the locals into the swing of things.

Alan Partridge-Tastic

It's not that simple Ly-ynne. Well, all right then, it is.

Outfit

◆ Blazer with gold buttons, precisely parted greying hair (get the talc out), chinos and wet lips.

Props

◆ Hanky.

◆ Copies of 'Bouncing Back' with stag's face on the front cover.

◆ Half-moon reading glasses on a chain for all of you (Larry Grayson eat your heart out).

◆ A job spec and interview questions for your new PA.

◆ Chocolate body paint.

Something for the stag

◆ Greying Shredded Wheat-look wig, Partridge style.

Challenges

◆ Play the air guitar and air drums to a song of your bucks' choice.

◆ Convince a garage or fast food joint to give you a free hot apple pie. Make sure they know *exactly* how warm it is by spitting out the first mouthful into your hand and exclaiming, 'It's hotter than the sun!'

◆ You're having a Partridge Bondathon moment. Make your favourite secret agent proud with your stealth-like manoeuvres to get to the bar.

◆ Reprimand a courting couple as they frolic in public. At the end of your tirade be sure to use the words, 'That's disgusting'.

◆ Lynne's had enough. Send your point man to round up some prospective recruits to interview for the role of your PA. Your bucks will have prepared the questions for you.

◆ Request that a lady of your bucks' choice paints your face with chocolate body paint and then gives you a kiss.

◆ Deliver these winning one-liners throughout the night:

– Jackanackanory.

– Back of the net.

– Cash back (with the one-armed bandit arm action).

– Daaaaaaan! (over the shoulder of whichever lady you're speaking to).

Activities

Check out the activity ideas and Alternative Directory for:

◆ Petrol stations (don't bother looking – there aren't any).

◆ The dogs.
◆ Canal boat trips.

Alternatives

◆ Britain is blessed with a plethora of real-life orange TV favourites to choose from: David 'cheap as chips' Dickinson, Des O'Connor (aging crooner and, inexplicably, young tottie magnet), or Dale 'Supermarket Sweep' Winton (a whiz with the nation's balls), to name but a few.

Stags in Drag – Cheerleaders

For some, it's any excuse to get dressed up as birds. So here you go – pom-poms, fake smiles, loose knicker elastic and high kicks at the ready.

Outfit

◆ Tight white T-shirts with a blown-up photo of the stag, plus the initial of his first name, on the front.

◆ White bobby socks, trainers, short pleated skirts.

◆ Wigs for the follicly challenged. Hair bands for the rest.

◆ American tan tights – essential for an authentic cheerleader.

◆ Fake boobs.

Props

◆ Pom-poms – all the same colour.

◆ A cheerleading chant for the main evening.

Something for the stag

◆ Pom-poms in silver or gold.

- Bright T-shirt with a slogan like 'Getting hitched' on the front.
- Lipstick-enhanced rosy cheeks and freckles drawn on with eyeliner.
- Definitely a long blonde wig with bunches.

Challenges

- You've been in training for months. Have a competition with a girl of your bucks' choice. The highest kick wins and you've got three chances each.
- Being around all those sports jocks has turned you into a bit of a heavy drinker. Challenge someone to a shot duel.
- Convince a girl to shake her pom-poms at you.
- You are a veritable dancing goddess. *American Beauty* had nothing on you. Give a woman a lap dance in return for a drink. Alternatively, your bucks will buy you a drink if you can convince her to give you a lap dance.
- You spend ages limbering up before a routine. Your point man will find you one or more girls to have a limbo-dancing contest with. Bucks will use their arms in place of the stick.

Activities

Check out the activity ideas and Alternative Directory for:

- schooldisco.com.

Other Starters for Themes

In principle, any theme can be developed in the same way as the ones featured, and even the challenges can be mixed and matched. Here are some starters to get you thinking.

Superheroes

Roll out the old favourites to relive your fantasies from the days when you were young enough for them to be clean. Bucks get the male heroes (Incredible Hulk, Superman, Spiderman, Batman, Robin, Iceman, He-Man and Captain Caveman), while the stag gets the joy of spinning into true Wonder Woman form. Alternatively, the stag gets to be the hero or heroine, while the bucks are all the villains (e.g. Joker, Riddler, Penguin, Cat Woman and Two Face for Batman).

Naval Officers

Has the stag ever wished he could impress someone by telling them he was a pilot? Well, the sight of able seamen or naval air force officers in uniform will certainly turn a few female heads. And you get the chance to set a challenge for the stag to sing 'You've Lost That Loving Feeling' to an unsuspecting girl-next-door-type in a bar. As his wingmen, you've got to support him in whatever he has to do.

Monkey Magic

Not what you'd imagine if you're a child of the 80s. In this instance, all the bucks dress up as monkeys and spend the evening chasing the stag, who is dressed like a banana, or Bananaman, around the town for the night.

Gangsters

A hobbyhorse's head, water pistols, trilby hats, violin cases and cotton wool balls for your mouths should do the trick. Again, if the stag's going to stand out, he's either got to be the Godfather or a gangster's moll. And if he's going in drag, fishnet tights are a must – his gems will never be the same again.

Spice Girls

Only really a winner if there are five of you. But who could resist the 'hi ci ya, hold tight' and high kicks of Ginger, Posh, Scary, Sporty and Baby? Wigs and a truckload of make-up a must.

Baywatch Boys

Not just for men with a physique to rival a bronzed Adonis. Prepare yourselves for lots of rescuing damsels in distress, cooling off in the hot sun with ice cubes, pec flexing, oiling up, and even resuscitation techniques. Plus the stag will look great as Pammy.

Latino Lovers

It's time to air your Cuban heels, satin shirts, excessive jewellery and slicked back locks for a night of rhythm, salsa forfeits and Casanova antics. The stag needs to stand out with a mega medallion, fetching tash and fake chest wig. Be warned, don't go to an official salsa club or you might find that you don't stand out as much as you'd hoped.

Action Men

If dog tags and *Die Hard* are more your style then this is for you. Don your face paint, army fatigues and white Bruce Willis vest, and practise your floor rolls. The only considerations are that you might either have problems getting in places or come up against some real squaddies that take it upon themselves to show you what's what.

Fame

You could lose friends with this one. Leg warmers, leggings or tight shorts, T-shirts with the sleeves torn off, and sweat bands. And with a frizzy wig and the right get-up, the stag should end up looking like Leo 'You make me feel like dancing' Sayer, ready to demonstrate a few 360-degree turns and split leaps during the night.

Alternative Stag Speech

This is your chance as the chief buck to deliver the unedited version of the wedding speech. You know, the kind of speech that, if uttered on the big day, could result in an epidemic of cardiac arrests among the more elderly guests and a strop-on by the bride.

As it's likely that the bucks all know the stag from different eras in his life, you've got a few options. You can: be a smug git and hog the whole subject of the alternative speech yourself, in preparation for the gruelling experience that lies ahead; amass a speech of great, albeit debauched, wit and anecdotes from all the research you'll be carrying out for the main speech anyway; or stage a *This is Your Life* speech, with you as Michael Aspel leading all the other stags into their tales. The Big Red Book memento is a nice touch too.

Take this opportunity to bring up tales of girls past, faux pas and deviances that the stag would rather forget, and reminisce over rites of passage that the wedding guests might never forgive him, or you, for. Avoid the tumbleweeds at the reception on the big day – get all the really dodgy material out of the way now.

Drinking Games

Everyone knows a drinking game or two. It just gets a bit hard to remember the rules when you've always ended up the worse for wear every time you played them. Here are a few to whet your appetite, although it's definitely worth pacing yourself to get the most out of your stag do, and your stag.

Just to clarify, for those of you that haven't left the house in the past twenty years, in terms of drinking fines a 'finger' is the width of your finger from the top of your beer level in your glass, usually about 2 cm worth of beer. Big hands? Bad luck. Nice for the ladies, but a handicap for drinking games. And remember, froth doesn't count.

Roles

Throwing some of the roles below into the equation should get everyone on track a bit quicker ...

Mr Chairman: This is the first position to be appointed because the Chairman hands out the rest of the roles unless they are won by other means. He can also issue random fines to anyone who has unreasonable requests, for example, repeatedly holding everyone up for toilet stops. He is the voice of reason in disputes and delivers the final ruling on appeals. Mr C could well be the stag, being as he's likely to get stitched up on every other score.

Mr Freeze: At any time he wants, Mr Freeze should strike an obvious pose. And not move. All other players must do the same as soon as they notice. The last one to stop moving has to down a two-finger fine. The recipient of the fine then becomes Mr Freeze, and so on.

Mr Thumbs: When he puts his right thumb on the table, other players must respond likewise. Left thumbs don't count. The last player to do so must down a two-finger fine and then becomes Mr Thumbs. Other variations are Mr Foot or Mr Head (steady), or for those of you who have never grasped the concept of the complete lack of pub or bar hygiene, Mr Tongue.

Mr Jive: When he stands up and dances, the other players must do the same. The last one up has to down a two-finger fine and becomes the new Mr Jive. Other variations on this one are Mr Air Guitar/Drums and Mr Dude (surfing the breakers).

Mr Rules: He covers those added extras, such as no pointing or

saying the word 'point' in any form, no saying the word 'drink', no right-hand drinking, no using first names, or only using pseudonyms in place of real names. Two-finger drinking penalty for all offenders.

Mr Weights and Measures: The best man. Keeps a track to make sure everyone's drinking their allotted fines and sets fines for new rules. Also enforces the 'drink while you think' rule. Tricky when your brain's turned to mush.

Nags

Tools of the trade:

◆ A packet of salted peanuts.

◆ A 'race' pint in the middle of the table.

◆ A fairly small group.

All the players sit around the table with the race pint in the middle. Each player has a 'nag' (a peanut) to race. One player makes a bet; the first to reach the bottom of the race pint wins, for example. You can make different bets each time so everyone gets a go at setting the stakes. On starter's orders all players drop their nags into the race pint and keep an eye on their own to see if they win or lose. In this case, the last one to reach the bottom of the pint or to not reach it at all has to down two fingers of their pint. All sorts of tactics can be involved, for example, peanuts drop at different rates depending on how much salt they have on them so players can lick it off to streamline their filly. Players can 'buy' another nag from the stable (the packet of peanuts) by drinking another two fingers. If a player's nag breaks in half while racing, that player must down their pint.

I Have Never ...

This can be played anywhere as long as the stag group is in some semblance of a circle. It is a good conversation starter if you are all static

Team Tactics

If you're planning on watching a team sport event during the weekend, allocate one or more of the sports players to each member of the stag party. Every time a player receives a mention by the commentator, scores, or even touches the ball, the lucky backer (buck or stag) must drink a one- or two-finger fine. Two could get a bit messy so it might be best to start with one, otherwise you might not see much more of the evening.

You can pretty much adapt this to anything you like, including all of you drinking a one- or two-finger fine every time someone who's not in the party says the words 'stag' or 'married' to any one of you.

too, like when you are waiting for your meal to turn up. One person is elected to begin. They start by saying 'I have never...' followed by something that they have never done. This must be a true statement. Anyone around the table who has done the deed then drinks a one-finger fine and so then you can interrogate them for the gory details. The game continues around the circle in the same way. A great ice-breaker but best not played with other halves at any time. Ever.

Matchbox Game

A simple game with fast results. The bucks need to sit in a circle around a flat surface, and take it in turns to throw a matchbox up in the air. Everyone must have a turn and the order is clockwise around the circle. How the matchbox lands each time it is thrown determines the drinking fine that needs to be taken or passed on to the next thrower round the circle. In short, if the matchbox lands on the:

◆ long edge, it accumulates a two-finger fine and passes to the next player;

◆ short edge, it accumulates four fingers of fine and passes to the next player, or the thrower gets to make up a new drinking rule (see the 'Roles' for ideas);

◆ large face, the player has to drink the accumulated fine and is checked by Mr Weights and Measures where necessary. The game only restarts when he has done this, so it's an incentive to do it quickly. If there is no fine then the matchbox carries on to the next player in the circle;

◆ floor, leg or anywhere other than the flat surface, the player has to neck whatever is left of their drink at that time.

Thrupennies

Another easy one, similar to the matchbox game. The bucks sit in a circle around a flat surface, and take it in turns to throw two coins up in the air. Everyone has a turn, and the order is clockwise around the circle. How the pennies land each time will determine the penalty:

◆ A head and a tail – the thrower is off the hook. The coins pass on to the next player without any penalty.

◆ Two heads – the player must drink a two-finger fine.

◆ Two tails – the player makes an additional rule or can choose to pass an immediate two-finger fine on to one of the players. Play still continues with the next player in the circle.

◆ Anywhere other than the flat surface, the player has to down whatever is left of their drink at that time before play continues.

Stags

A good one to warm everyone up without having to get completely wasted. This is the age-old Vikings game adapted to stag antlers instead. Sit round a table and kick-off with your stag. He puts his thumbs to his temples with his hands splayed out upright like antlers and shoulders thrust back as he assumes the role of chief stag. The bucks on either side of him must also have antlers and throw their heads forward and puff to mimic young bucks rutting. Relatively quickly, the chief stag then 'throws' his role across to another one of the group by flicking his wrists to point his antlers in that direction. The new chief stag immediately puts his hands in place for antlers and thrusts his shoulders back, while the players on either side of him also instantly become the rutting stags in support. Whenever anyone messes up, takes too long to get it together or indeed stops rutting, they must drink a two-finger fine. The 'throws' get faster to force players to keep up and stay focused. The best way for this game to work is to add in some extra roles: Mr Thumbs and Mr Freeze at least. Any additional roles are higher up on the pecking order than the chief stag and rutting bucks so you will really need to stay on the ball to avoid fines.

Play Your Numbers Right

You'll need to be in fine voice for this one. And you don't need anything else to play it. The stag starts the game by saying 'one', then someone else must take the initiative to say 'two' and so on, so that you are counting as a group. There's no order for who has to follow who. The twist is that if two people say the same number at the same time, they must both drink two fingers and the numbers start again at 'one'. If no one says anything at all, the player that said the last number can take the prerogative to shout 'nil'. Then he can give a two-finger fine to whichever player he chooses (probably the really quiet one who thinks he's being sneaky trying to sit this one out). If anyone says a number at the same time as 'nil' is said, they automatically get a two-finger fine anyway. Invariably, Mr Chairman also ends up coming into play to rule on reasonable wait times.

Fuzzy Duck

It doesn't take a genius to work out what you'll end up saying here, but it's still a good option after a few drinks have slowed your brain up. The stag and bucks need to be in a circle to start. The premise is that the first player says 'Fuzzy Duck' and the person on his left then chooses whether to carry on saying 'Fuzzy Duck', in which case play continues, or 'Does he?' in which case play changes direction. Once the direction changes to be anti-clockwise, the next player has the choice of saying 'Ducky Fuzz', for play to continue, or 'Does he?' to change direction again. It's good to get it flying around the table and not looking at the person who's meant to go next to make it more likely that they will screw up their turn. Anyone that misses their cue or says the wrong thing must drink a two-finger fine, so obviously speed is of the essence.

Again, some of the extra roles thrown in for good measure make it even trickier.

Dark Horses

This is another great game to help to bond your group of bucks and also tests your stag's knowledge of his friends. This game requires a little preparation and someone to play quizmaster to pose the questions to the stag. Ask each of your bucks to write down a couple of rarely disclosed facts about themselves without telling anyone else. These can be things they have done or secrets about themselves that your stag will not necessarily know. Gather up all the bits of paper and then read them out to the stag one by one. Tell him that each is a fact about someone in the group and then he has to guess who you are talking about or face a fine. The more risqué or amusing the facts, the better.

Skeletons in the Closet

Tools of the trade:

◆ One pint.

◆ One double tequila.

Both drinks are put in front of the stag. All the bucks have clues about the same someone from the stag's past. Ideally, an ex-girlfriend that will be tricky to guess, which is obviously easier if he's had more girlfriends than Monica Lewinsky's had cigars. Otherwise it might need to be an ex-flirtation. The stag can buy clues from the bucks at one finger of the pint a pop. If he can't guess the mystery skeleton by the end of the pint, he also has to down the tequila. If he does guess the skeleton, he can pass the tequila fine on to whomever he likes. Not recommended for more than one skeleton if you want to see your stag survive past 8 p.m.

Stag Wave

If you invoke the stag wave rule, it means that at any point during the drinking session anyone can call a stag wave. The ground rule is that everyone must have at least half a pint left at the time. Once declared, the caller has to down what's left of their pint, and everyone else must follow suit and place the empty glass upside down on their head. No exceptions. And it serves you right if you thought this was a good suggestion when you know you've got complete beer monsters in your party.

Alternative Activities – for Day and Night

Stretch out that weekend. And make way, the lads are on tour and looking for action. Whether you're looking for a rib tickler, ball tightener or to kick back and chill out, feast your porkies on these.

Activities are listed alphabetically. Each has been given an Alternative Stag star rating from 1 to 5 (where 5 is best), based on novelty value, adrenaline rush and suitability for a stag weekend. As a starting point for contact details on a range of these activities, see the links in the text or look for a listing by city in the Alternative Directory.

Abseiling ★★★

A controlled backwards descent from the top of something reeeally high up, while tied to something strong. Involves walk/climb of fear to point of departure, deep breath and backwards tip, walking in reverse down incredibly high fascia while almost at right angles to it. Possibly a bit of bouncing if you're up to it. And not forgetting kissing the ground.

Air Shows ★

Not particularly inspirational, but not bad for a 'big boys toys' day out with beers. Brilliant if your idea of fun is looking up people's noses. You can pay to have short joyrides in helicopters and small planes when you're there too. Only an option for a summer stag do.

See www.flyingzone.co.uk/airshows/airshows.htm for a list of UK air show dates.

Amusement Parks ★★

Britain is blessed with a fair few amusement parks. Great for a top day out to get the adrenaline pumping in advance of a stag's Saturday night. The reason it's only got two stars? Well, it's hardly original, but don't let that stop you. The only other drawback is that if there's a big group of you without any formal organisation it can be tricky to get anything done and keep everyone together.

Archery ★★★

You could have your eye out with that! OK, so you're not Robin 'arrow splitter' Hood, but if your stag's a poser, this could be the action you're after. Just watch out for rogue arrows and shot-to-bits upper arm tendons the next day.

Beer Tasting ★

For stags who love beer more than action, there's the national beer festival at Olympia in London every year in August, but failing that a good beer-swilling day at a local brewery or scrumpy farm is an option whatever the weather. Just don't bank on making it a 'night to remember' if you're starting early.

Bungee Jumping ★★★★

The time has come to arrange for the stag to have his life flash before his eyes as a rite of passage before he enters into the world of marriage. This is an amazingly exhilarating experience none of you should miss, and it'll make sure all of you are pumped up so that your night will be a sure-fire winner.

Camping ★

Not necessarily everyone's ideal but, if you're on a really tight budget, amusing the locals with your fancy dress themes and games followed by a well-planned night around a campfire can be great. Naturally, to protect the innocent, it's best to avoid pitching your tents alongside a family campervan; you don't want them to shock you, after all.

Canal Boats ★★★

Whether it's the Norfolk Broads, the Thames or the Grand Union Canal, a day out or even a weekend is a right laugh. Dock up at pubs en route and chill out on deck with a couple of beers. Plus, as long as you don't pick a canal that needs to be dredged to clear out all the shopping trolleys, you can always live dangerously and go for a dip. See www. britishwaterways.co.uk or www.canalboats.co.uk for UK routes.

Canoeing and Kayaking ★★★

If you're inexperienced, it's probably best not to go off any ten-metre-high waterfalls, as broken bones take longer than four weeks to heal, and drowning is even more of a blight. Britain has a wealth of centres offering canoe and kayak tours to suit any ability, and they provide the equipment which makes them the preferred option.

Castle or Cottage Weekends ★★★

For a more lad-focused and less flirtatious stag night, hire a castle, cottage, mill or tower for the weekend. Again, it's good to put effort into a theme or at least a plan for the weekend. Pick something that is associated with the stag and go from there. If you're flash, you might even want to go to Europe in the winter to hire a ski chalet with roaring log fires and après ski to contend with. Check out ads in the weekend supplements because details are updated regularly and so are policies regarding stag parties ...

Caving and Potholing ★★★

Not up everyone's street. And it involves burrowing around underground in tight wet spaces rather than being above ground doing something a bit more flash. But if none of you have been before, it will be a new challenge for you to overcome together. Just bear in mind that confined spaces have limited appeal if you're claustrophobic or have a hangover.

Circle Line Pub Crawl, London ★★

Simple concept. Impossible to do. For a serious drinking session, shell out a whole four quid something on a London zone one tube pass and cruise the circle line. Do what it says on the packet – one pub stop at each tube station on the route. The other option is to go for the Monopoly board challenge, according to whichever city you're in. You don't stand a chance.

Circus School ★★★★

It's certainly different. And definitely good for a laugh. For some crazy antics and death-defying skills, roll up and enjoy the show. Learn to juggle with more than two balls, master the trapeze, and demonstrate your acrobatic and acro-balance abilities. Check out www.chillisauce.co.uk/active/lazy/index.php for more info.

Clay Pigeon Shooting ★★★★★

Pull! Never mind the battered shoulder from the kickback, there's something very powerful about firing a shotgun and smelling the gun smoke. In an age of strict gun control, this is the 'safe' option and is a brilliant feeling. It also allows a bit of friendly competition between the lads.

Comedy Clubs ★★

Depending on whom you speak to, some people go to comedy clubs all the time, others still think it's alternative. Either way, this is a good Friday night option to get everyone off to a fun start without breaking the bank, and there's usually a DJ and dancing until late to boot.

Digger and JCB Racing ★★★★★

Don your yellow hard hat. This calls for some serious bum-crack display. A variation on the usual motor sport experiences, you get to have your very own alternative race. And enjoy yourselves while you can – as workmen in training, every half an hour there will no doubt be an obligatory twenty-minute tea break.

The Dogs ★★

The haaaa-rrrre is ooon the moooove! A visit to the poor man's nags is an opportune moment to air your cloth cap if you're a closet pigeon fancier. Alternatively, you could get with the times for a classic Friday night warm-up before the official stag night. Chicken in a basket, cheap beer, loose women and real ale all beckon. See under all cities in the directory or look up www.thedogs.co.uk.

Fire Walking ★★

If your stag's getting cold feet, take his mind off things with a challenging fire walk. Once he's done this, he'll know he can achieve anything. An ideal Sunday roast although, because most of the courses are based on self-belief, it is a bit touchy-feely. To read more, see www.firewalkingschool.com.

Fishing ★

Get your tackle out and wait for a bite. Alternatively, kick back and relax. Because, let's face it, there's nothing very exciting about fishing. But it is a tepid excuse for a chilled out, laid back, cold beers kind of summer's day. Just steer clear of anyone who looks like they've staked out a patch of river for some serious angling. When they are properly baited, you will realise that they're not quite so sporting as they lynch you with a barbed hook at ten paces. See www.activity-scotland.co.uk/fishing.htm and www.goflyfishing.co.uk.

Flying ★★

Planes, gliders, microlights or helicopters. Not bad if it's your stag's lifelong dream. But not really a male bonding exercise, so it's probably not a good idea for everyone to do it. Surprise the stag with his flight, chill out in the officers' mess while he's gone, and then get on with the day.

Gliding ★★

Leave your stomach behind as you make your rapid ascent into the air at a 45-degree angle, courtesy of a towrope. A brown paper bag is a handy accessory, but once the lurch up is out of the way, you'll have the chance to experience soaring and riding the thermals for the bargain price of about £25–£35 a go. The best flights are mid-morning, just as the thermals get going (yes, we do have them in Britain), and before the turbulence and winds cause any disruption.

Golf ★

Don your plus fours and Pringle jumper – the greens are calling. If you're not all practised golfers, you'll have to opt for the public courses or risk the wrath of the professionals. Not bad for a small stag party as course etiquette means groups are usually limited to four people. Not so hot when there are loads of you because you'll end up in lots of small groups and won't see each other for about four hours on an 18-holer.

If you are prepared to go to town and base your stag weekend at La Manga or Gleneagles, then bump the star rating up to a three.

Hang Gliding ★★★★

Involves running to the edge of a sheer drop and keeping on going, while putting all your faith in a large kite to stop you from dropping out of the sky like a stone. A few of you can go at once so it's good for a group activity, and it doesn't take all day either. If you're going to do this it's wise to take it fairly easy the night before because, although it's classed as exhilarating, chunder might rain from the heavens. Be prepared for bruises.

Helicopters ★★★

Not just for flash gits. If you're not up to a lesson to pilot a helicopter yourself, there's always a helicopter ride. Tourist destinations often have sightseeing tours, and some local airfields offer leisure flights.

Horse Racing ★★

Classy. And cool. The sport of kings could leave you broke but you will have a great day out all the same. Local courses have races sporadically throughout the year. Check out the sporting fixtures chapter to find dates for the classic events. It's also an opportunity to show off your finery, so get togged up and choose from hobnobbing it in the grandstand or grabbing your patch of ringside turf for free at some of the meets.

Hot Air Ballooning ★★

Definitely one of the more civilised options for a chilled out, champagne filled kind of day as you soar over the countryside. Shut your eyes and sit at the bottom of the basket if you're afraid of heights … you cravat-wearing pansy.

It's a Knockout ★★★★

Be prepared – this is pricey and, with some companies, you need to be able to supply your own field and 3,000 gallons of water! This really limits the option to very large groups; perhaps a few joint stag dos, or even a 'shag' do (see the 'Shags and Hags' chapter). Take a trip back in time to the days when TV spent a lot of money on shows with people in fancy dress doing strange activities and bombarding each other with goo.

Jet Skiing ★★

Action toys with motors. The show-off factor is worth it alone. Just don't spend too much time on the day with your eyes closed imagining yourself on clear blue waters, smelling of coconut oil. You'll crash.

Karting ★★★

Not amazingly alternative, but bloody good fun all the same. Race each other round a track to determine who has ultimate supremacy. You'll need to book in advance to definitely get the same timeslot for all of you and ensure it will be a testosterone-fuelled evening.

Laser Quest ★★

Living in the 80s. Inspired by the likes of *Terminator* and *Robocop*, a generation of lads headed for the dark, indoor corridors at the back of bowling alleys to fire rays of light at each other. Ooooh. It's paintball without the cold mud and bruises. Or paint for that matter. But still good for a trip down memory lane.

Medieval Banquet ★★

'Enry the eighth you might not be, but no doubt you could be tempted to get garbed up in tights and tear away at a turkey leg to impress the damsels. Beats sitting in the pub as a Friday night possibility anyway.

Motor Experience Days ★★★★★

Speed. Style. Sex. If your stag considers himself to be a driver-playboy extraordinaire along the lines of Eddie Irvine but is really more of a boy racer, then look no further – you've found the ideal activity. From Ferrari or Lotus handling to skidpan driving, 4WD challenges to high-speed cornering, and military vehicles to rally driving. This will blow your socks off. It is not that cheap, but it's definitely all about big boys' toys and will be an experience none of you will forget in a hurry.

Mountain Biking ★★

Now, there are two ways of looking at this. The 50 percenters just pedal around on a mountain bike and use artistic licence to describe what they do. The 100 percenters are after the kind of downhill hell-for-leather death rides that make your jaws and buttocks clench until they ache. Take your pick. Either way, this is a challenge for a group of hungover, pen pushing, office lads who only associate the word 'exercise' with something they used to bunk off at school. For more information, call a bike shop in the area you're interested in – contacts can be found in magazines such as *MBUK* or *MBR*. They'll have an up-to-date list of local trails and will be able to tell you about organised rides for all levels of ability.

Murder Mystery ★

You can either go on an organised weekend or buy the box set and do it yourself. Whodunnit? It could only be Miss Scarlet in the PVC basque, with the handcuffs in the dungeon. Not as exciting as it sounds but can be a good laugh with the right crowd. See www.murdermysteryevents.com and www.murdermostfoul.co.uk for examples.

Outdoor Activity Centres ★★★★★

Whether you're looking for an action-packed day or weekend, these centres offer a range of activities from abseiling, clay pigeon shooting, quad bikes, archery, horse riding, climbing, blindfolded driving, canoeing, ropes courses, home-made raft racing and orienteering, among other things. Traditionally popular for team-building days, these are a great laugh for a stag do and a lot of them cater specifically to stag and hen parties.

Outdoor Concerts ★

In terms of a day out, this is chilled and can be classy if you want. If you just go along with a picnic, it's not really that alternative. But you can go to town and take a table, tablecloth, silverware, candelabra, optics shelf, banquet, and dress in DJs to do the day in style. Lots of stately homes and castles around the country boost their incomes by putting on these concerts. See www.performingarts.co.uk.

Paintballing ★★★★

An excellent group day out. Can get a bit pointless when paintball geeks get out their own mega-guns and buy up more ammo than is humanly possible to fire in half a day, so book up in advance and see if you can take over a whole course. Or at least ask to be pitted against a team that are also in it for a laugh rather than to prove their Rambo status. If in doubt, check your opponents' arms for train-track scars where they've stitched up their own wounds in the past.

Parachuting ★★★★★

A tandem jump is great for a one-day activity. With only 30 minutes training, you all take to the skies, just about staying conscious because your blood supply has been cut off somewhere around your nether regions by the parachute ties. Thankfully, each of you is strapped to someone who does know what they're doing, and when that side door opens and the wind rushes past your face so fast it's hard to breathe, adrenaline is coursing through your veins. Then you're out of the plane, free-falling at speeds of 120 mph for about 7,000 feet, depending on your jump. There's a reason why they call it 'ground rush'. Absolutely exhilarating. See www.tandemjump.co.uk and www.jumpwithus.co.uk.

Parasailing ★★

Essentially, a parachute ride launched from the ground as you're towed along behind a speedboat. It's good fun on holiday or in really small groups. A bit of an adrenaline rush, and definitely alternative, but it's hardly a group activity and so not ideal for a stag party unless you're all happy sitting on the beach while the stag has his turn. Not likely during a British summer!

Polo Clubs ★★★★

You might think this is not a madly exciting day out unless you're interested in watching a bunch of toffs cantering around a field. But you don't have to settle for being a spectator any more. Sign your stag group up for a full or half-day polo training session where you will have some brief training and then pit your skills against each other, or another stag or hen party. You even get a trophy at the end of it all, with a glass of bubbly, naturally. Previous riding experience is not necessary. See www.polo.co.uk or www.hpa-polo.co.uk for more information.

Powerboats ★★

Hang on to your wigs while a skilled boatman whizzes you through the surf. If you don't fancy a whole day of sailing, this is a great compromise. Half an hour of crashing through the ocean waves Crockett and Tubs (*Miami Vice*) style, before heading back to find your sea legs and stagger to the pub. In fancy dress, this is a perfect start to an 80s or *Baywatch* themed night.

Quad Bikes ★★★

What can possibly be better than a motorbike with two wheels? Well, if you can't actually ride a motorbike, then a bike with four wheels is the winner. Although a few of you may have already tried this, it's a great opportunity to get some friendly competition going between the stag and bucks. Speed and finish lines tend to guarantee that will happen anyway. And it's not only affordable, but also available throughout the UK.

Recording Studio ★★★

Was your stag always convinced he was robbed of a rock career? Did he strut in front of his mirror with an air guitar and ad hoc microphone giving his rock idol his best, as it were? A recording studio experience is definitely alternative and with a CD of your labours to take home you will have a great memento of the weekend, not only for posterity, but also as wedding speech ammo. Perfect. Search for recording studio gifts on the Internet, or gift experience companies such as www.memorisethis.com will organise it for you.

Rock and Ropes ★★★

Death-defying leaps from high platforms. Not for the faint-hearted or vertigo sufferers. While you might relish the idea of being in the middle of nowhere, you no longer need to go out into the wilds to rock climb or suspend yourself at a precarious height. Some nice chaps and chapesses have put together ropes courses especially for groups like you, in convenient locations close to towns.

Sailing ★★★★

Relax and enjoy the ocean waves. There's only one way to do this – a private charter for the day and do it in style. Cruise the Solent and have lunch on the Isle of Wight or tack along the coastline. This is a superb day out in the sun. Live like international playboys. Not the cheapest option but brilliant. If you've got at least one or two experienced sailors, or can afford to pay for crew, you might even want to enter an amateur sailing race to go the extra mile.

Scuba Diving ★

The eighth wonder of the world – the ocean. But the likelihood is, you're not going to be diving in clear blue waters on coral reefs. If that is the case, you can also go on courses in pools and lakes, or if you hold the relevant certificates, gravel pits and the North Sea are also your oysters. Just remember, not everyone can do it, especially if they suffer from asthma, and it's not really suitable for getting the banter going.

Shooting Range ★★★

The UK takes its firearms regulations very seriously so, while a day out at a shooting range is a lot of fun, large groups are in danger of getting turned away – and if they catch even a whiff of alcohol, you're scuppered. As you would imagine, you won't be let loose with a 12-gauge shotgun or Walther PPK, but you will be able to test your target skills with an air rifle. Obviously a spot of competition doesn't hurt either. If you're after something a little 'heavier', you'll have to go to foreign shores.

Skiing and Snowboarding ★★★

Depending on your budget and location, you've got few options. At the cheapest end of the scale there is dry slope skiing, along with snowdomes, where real snow is created for indoor short ski runs. And then there's proper resort skiing, where you can take the opportunity to take over a whole chalet and go to town on a premium five-star stag do.

Stock Car and Banger Racing ★★★★★

Smell the burning rubber and oil, and be deafened by the roaring engines as drivers smash into each other around the track. The danger element makes this an exciting night out. But why stop there? Get your stag behind the wheel in the rookie banger class – all you need is an old wreck that you are willing to thrash and trash. See www.stockcar.co.uk.

Strip Clubs ★★★

Hardly alternative, but it could be the stag's last chance before the thumb print on the top of his head really starts to show. There's no getting away from it. For many, a stag weekend just wouldn't be complete without some visual T&A stimulation. It's just a shame we don't have one-pound notes to fold any more. Coins can be tricky.

Sumo ★★★

Don your Pampers and eat for Britain. Or, alternatively, borrow the sweaty padding provided and grunt like a pig. You get to walk like a fat but incredibly well-hung John Wayne, and throw your mates around with bouts of thigh slapping thrown in for good measure. Go on, make Clive James proud. Search the web for details of sumo and other inflatable activities, such as gladiator combat, bungee running, space hopper racing and giant games.

Surfing ★★

While surfing in Swansea or Cornwall isn't quite as glamorous as California or Hawaii, it is cheap, on the doorstep, and there aren't any man-eating sharks either. It's definitely a skill to master. In the meantime, enjoy a hearty laugh at your mates' misfortunes before copping a face full of salt and foam yourself.

Survival Courses ★★★★

Action men, eat your heart out. Not ones to miss an opportunity to make some cash, army hardnuts have developed a weekend wilderness survival course for all those masochists out there. Allegedly, it is great fun, so if smearing your face with sheep droppings, pushing yourself to your physical limits, sleeping in bivvie bags, hiking for miles and clambering over large obstacles is your thing, then go for it. In old Soviet states, you can even get the chance to fire off a few rounds from a Kalashnikov. The ultimate in male bonding.

Swimming ★★

None of your namby-pamby stuff. If you're in London for your stag night, check out the Serpentine swimming club for the ultimate hangover cure. They're a bunch of fruit-loopers that take a dip in the Serpentine Lake in Hyde Park every Saturday morning at 8 a.m. to keep their peckers up. See www.serpentineswimmingclub.com.

Tank Driving ★★★★

Don your dog tags, it's time to play with the hard-core toys. Go on, Action Man, see what it feels like to be inside one of these things and handling the controls, without running the risk of getting signed-up.

Tenpin Bowling ★

There are only two legitimate reasons to sink this low for a stag night – you are truly broke, or the stag is a wet dishrag.

Water-Skiing and Wakeboarding ★★★

Despite mouthfuls of water, ripped shoulder tendons and a home-made enema if you go down with your legs open, this is great fun. And, being as this green and pleasant land gets more than its fair share of water, it's also very accessible. Just check with venues before you go as nearly all of them are seasonal.

White-Water Rafting ★★★★★

A brilliant group activity. Make no mistake, this can be dangerous. And the challenge of negotiating the white water, while all staying in the raft, really pulls everyone together to work as a team. After that, team tactics for the evening will be a cinch. It's bound to get you all off to a flying start for the stag do – after a day's rafting, a well-planned night can't fail to impress. Book early for Saturday slots, as they are popular for all the right reasons.

Windsurfing ★★

A high cool rating is offset by the fact that unless you're experienced, this is not as easy as it looks. You could spend the whole day just getting away from the shoreline, and if you turn the wrong way into the wind you'll know about it. That said, if you've got a smallish group and can get an introductory lesson together, then it will no doubt leave you with some anecdotes to reminisce over. You might even develop a passion for it. Stranger things happen at sea …

Wine Tasting and Vineyard Tours ★★

Fancy yourself as a wine connoisseur? Or just a wino? Ideal if you'd like to know more about your tipple before you neck it and want some daytime drinking with a difference. The downside is that the vineyards are out of town so you'll need to be organised about getting there. One short cut is to visit London's 'Vinopolis' wine museum on the South Bank to sample their fare and then pop down to the riverside pubs for the rest of the day. See www.english-wine.com.

Zorbing ★★★

For a truly bizarre experience, strap your stag into a giant inflatable ball and throw him down a hill. No, this isn't because you've had enough of him going on about his missus-to-be. It's known as zorbing and, strangely, it is catching on. Introduced from New Zealand, the experienced sensation is supposed to be close to feeling weightless. You can have up to three people in a zorb per run, so the rest of you can join in by having a go or even lying in the path of the approaching zorb to ensure your stag has an eventful roll. See www.zorbsouth.co.uk.

Alternative Events Calendar – Home and Away

Throughout the year there are a host of events to be considered for your stag weekend. Here are a range of reasons to get away, whatever your budget.

JANUARY

Fiesta of St Paul – San Pablo de los Montes, Spain

Believe it or not, the women of the town are happy to go along with this festival, which strips away decades of feminist achievements. For the whole of the carnival day, men can indulge themselves and go around lifting up girls' skirts at will, with no repercussions. Only one man has an unenviable deal – 'la Madre Cochina' (the Old Bat). This is a guy in drag, along the lines of a pantomime dame and, strangely, the local men seem more interested in badgering this much-harangued individual than checking out the undies and pruning techniques of the local women. Interesting.

Web: www.tourspain.es

Hahnenkamm Men's Downhill Ski Race Weekend – Kitzbuhel, Austria

Part of the Alpine Skiing World Cup, this is one of the most thrilling and glamorous events of the winter sports calendar. Fly out on the Friday for a day's skiing before the festivities kick in. The town of Kitzbuhel comes alive for the weekend, swarming with lots of male skiers, but also the legions of female admirers that follow them here. Result. The celebratory spirit is infectious and great for a stag do.

Web: www.hahnenkamm.com

Up-Helly-Aa – Shetland Islands, Scotland

If you want to get back to basics and have the option of dressing in sacking with big horns then check out the Up-Helly-Aa event. The locals go all out to recreate the Viking fire festival with a parade of over 900 people dressed as Vikings, complete with flaming torches and a full-size replica longboat as the centrepiece. Then, after all that effort, they torch the boat in a huge bonfire and while the poor boat maker sobs into the night, the sky is lit up with fireworks. The amazing atmosphere created by the fire, music and boozing Scots carries on into a night to remember.

Web: www.visitshetland.com/events/events.html

The Bommel Festival – Ronse, Belgium

Historically, Ronse was a place of pilgrimage for the mentally ill in the Middle Ages. Well, some of them must have settled here and played a part in setting up this celebration of the Epiphany. Generally the festival has the usual drinking and celebratory spirit surrounding these kinds of days with parades, local beer (brewed by the monks), food and entertainment, but it also has a few more bizarre offerings. One of these, on the Saturday, is the oversized costumed characters that entertain the crowds as foreplay, and then lay into each other with no restraint. Naturally, the Saturday is known as 'Crazy Monday'. Not quite Disney. And all highly amusing.

Web: www.visitflanders.com

FEBRUARY

Venetian Ball – Venice, Italy

Held during the ten days leading up to Ash Wednesday, this is the occasion to don your glad rags and fancy dress. The world-renowned masked ball is spectacular. The streets, canals and piazzas come alive with the throngs of partying people from all over the world – and they wonder why Venice is sinking. Shish. Needless to say, accommodation is in demand, so book up early to avoid disappointment.

Web: www.venicecarnival.com

Viking Festival – York, UK

If you weren't able to make the Up-Helly-Aa festival in January, then this runs a close second in terms of Viking events. It seems that people just love dressing up and beating the living daylights out of each other whenever they get a chance. At this festival, commemorating a Saxon/Viking battle in the tenth century, enthusiasts from all over the UK travel to York. They stage re-enactments of battles in full Viking and Saxon warrior kits, have longboat races on the Ouse, and act like oafs. In true Viking style, with passions riding high, the day can often get out of hand, which results in a fair few injuries. Always amusing, as long as you're not directly involved. A good day out for watching the action and swilling beer from the sidelines, plus York has all the usual nightlife you'd associate with a major city and university town.

Web: www.yorkshire-tourist-board.org.uk

Daytona 500 NASCAR Race – Daytona Beach, Florida, USA

While the Daytona 500 is the most well known race, the Daytona race events actually span a whole week. The cars race down the beach, and this meet is infamous because it attracts celebrities, motor enthusiasts, and bikini-clad bimbos alike. Florida is the party state of the US and in the spring months expect to see 'spring fever' from a lot of partygoers who haven't seen the sun for a while. The action begins with the Bud

Shootout, followed by the Twin 125 qualifying races, the BUSCH Grand National race and, finally, the Daytona 500. Watch out for action on and off the track.

Web: www.daytonaintlspeedway.com

Carnaval – Cadiz, Spain

Carnaval is celebrated all across Spain in the week running up to Shrove Tuesday. But Cadiz really knows how to do it. Here, the festival is extended to cover an additional weekend and people travel from miles around to come to this infamous party. Fancy dress is the order of the day and the spirit is very much alcohol enriched, further enhancing the great entertainment provided by bands, dancers, the parade and individual street artists. Accommodation gets booked up well in advance, so either get your butt into gear a couple of months ahead of time, or resign yourself to travelling in from a nearby town along with a lot of the other revellers.

Web: www.cadizturismo.com

Carnaval – Cologne (Köln), Germany

In the build-up to Ash Wednesday, the whole city kicks off for a week-long festival culminating in three final days of 24-hour partying in the Old Town. The Germans show the results of their fine beer-making skills, bands play, everyone seems to get into the spirit by dressing in fancy dress, and flirting is the order of the day. It is popular with visitors, but it is nowhere near as touristy as the Munich Oktoberfest. A bunch of lads in fancy dress should fit right in. Not to be missed.

Web: www.koeln.de

MARCH

St Patrick's Day – Ireland, New York or Chicago

We all know the Irish pride in being up for the craic. Visit pretty much any Irish city to join in the festivities or, if you want to go further afield, check out New York or even Chicago. The yanks go nuts for anything Irish, even if half of them can't point out Ireland on a map. New York has a huge population of Irish ex-pats to stir up the fun, while Chicago, not to be outdone, dyes the city river green as part of the celebrations.

Web: www.stpatricksday.ie/cms

Glasgow International Comedy Festival – Glasgow, Scotland

Not as well known as its sister festival in Edinburgh in August, and that means that there are fewer crowds, less hype and less price hiking too. Forget the 'Glasgow kiss'. This is a really underrated city in the UK and has a great nightlife and activities to support that. The comedy festival attracts a lot of the usual favourites on the circuit and also provides a forum for budding talent. Often runs into April too.

Web: www.glasgowcomedyfestival.com

Las Fallas – Valencia, Spain

Another infamous Spanish festival. This time, each neighbourhood sponsors the creation of a massive papier-mâché sculpture, called a 'fallas'. These can take up to a year to build and are erected overnight on street corners so that on 15 March the town awakes to a surreal exhibit of huge, magnificent and often satirical figures from politics, local culture or the world of celebrities. So, basically, the likelihood is that you won't know who many of them are but that shouldn't make a difference to your overall experience. The partying goes on for days, with street entertainment, paella-cooking frenzies, parades, music, bullfights and incredible nightly fireworks displays. Although Valencia is generally seen as the best example of the festival, Las Fallas is also celebrated in Benidorm.

Web: www.fallas.com (Spanish language only) and
www.turisvalencia.es

Ivrea Orange Festival – Ivrea, Italy

Held in the week running up to Shrove Tuesday, the exuberant nature of the event means it's gaining in popularity and the locals are passionate about it. Traditionally, the orange fight that runs for the last three days of the festival is for the citizens of Ivrea to re-enact their battle for freedom against Napoleon. Or citrus fruits. It's not really clear. But the kindly folk of the town have made it possible for anyone to become an honorary citizen of Ivrea for a day in order to join one of the makeshift orange-throwing teams. The aim of the game is to hit the hooded 'baddies' riding around the town on horse-drawn carriages, and there are even rules to prevent anarchy breaking out. The evening events include copious amounts of alcohol and a bonfire centrepiece in the town square. To top it all off, the locals really get into things by donning full fancy dress, one-armed Napoleonic apparel being a favourite.

Web: www.carnevalediivrea.it/defaulteng.shtm

Hong Kong Sevens – Hong Kong

For rugby fanatics, this is a pilgrimage that must be made at least once in your life. The three-day Sevens tournament features the top teams from around the world in faster, more furious games. Top it off with a day at Happy Valley Races to watch fanatical old ladies rub their hands in glee as they fleece you of your well-earned beer money.

Web: www.hksevens.com.hk

APRIL

Jazz and Heritage Festival – New Orleans, USA

N'Awlins, as the locals call it, is the city of cooool and the home of jazz. Nice. Also famous for its chilled vibe, Cajun food, sexy dancing, paddle steamers on the Mississippi and southern-style hospitality, the city plays host to Jazzfest, running for two weekends every spring. Stages all over town host acts from traditional jazz to blues, folk, gospel and electric jazz to name but a few. Again, you'll need to book in advance because the festival is now attracting about half a million visitors, and becoming more popular and diverse every year. Make sure you try the local 'Hurricane' cocktail delicacy while you're there – it is lethal.

Web: www.nojazzfest.com

Queen's Day – Amsterdam, The Netherlands

If you think Amsterdam is a party city on any other day of the year, you need to experience Queen's Day. Usually around the last weekend of April, the festival is laid on for the Queen's official birthday, and it keeps her very popular indeed. The canals are jammed with boats cruising the waterways, albeit it very slowly, and the streets are packed with a real carnival atmosphere. The city's squares and parks play host to stages for free music concerts, and beer and food is sold at the kerbside. Everyone gets completely slaughtered (the Dutch being one of the few nationalities to rival the Brits in terms of drinking) and amazingly there's rarely any trouble. Although that could be down to the other local produce on offer. To top it all off, the Dutch show their true colours by opting for orange attire or fancy dress for the day.

Web: www.visitamsterdam.nl

MAY

Cheese Rolling – Randwick, UK and Brockworth, UK

Every year, grown men and women hurl themselves down a very steep hill with no thought for their own safety – only of the coveted prize. Yes, they risk life and limb for a lump of cheese. Granted, it is a large lump of cheese, but it's still just cheese. On the last bank holiday weekend in May, they gather at Coopers Hill in Brockworth, and in Randwick. And a couple of hours later, at least a handful of them are in casualty for treatment to suspected broken bones. In an effort to cut down on the injuries, organisers have brought the start time forward from 3 p.m. to noon so that competitors don't have quite as long to get bevvied up and 'invincible' prior to any participation. Enlightening to watch if you're in that part of the world anyway, but probably best not to compete when you've all got to be at a wedding in a few weeks.

Web: www.visit-glos.org.uk and www.heartofenglandtouristboard.co.uk

Bantry Mussels Festival – Bantry, Ireland

Ideal for a stag weekend that is not activity packed but is chilled out with lots of good humour, food and drink. The townsfolk have taken the local delicacy and combined it with the national pint to form the basis of the Bantry Bay Mussels Festival – that is, mussels and stout. Running over the course of three days, the festival gets off to a comforting start with cooking competitions culminating in a sumptuous seafood spread. Before you've taken your first bite, you're bound to find a pint of stout in your hand, and thereafter you might as well wave goodbye to your stomach for the next few days. You never will know if it was the free mussels or the drink that did it, and nor will you care. And just so that you can keep a record of what day it is, there's also a firework display on the Saturday night.

Web: www.bantrymusselfair.ie

Kattenstoet – Ypres, Belgium

Kattenstoet is the perfect excuse to go somewhere for whatever reason. Every three years on 11 May the good folk of Ypres, for reasons best known to themselves, dress up as giant cats during the festival of Kattenstoet, a marvellously eccentric hangover from medieval times.

Web: www.visitflanders.com

The Cat Laughs Comedy Festival – Kilkenny, Ireland

Home of a great pint and now Kilkenny gives us a celebrated comedy festival bringing together popular comedians and fresh faces from the Irish and UK circuits. Brewery tours at Murphy's are an optional extra.
Web: www.thecatlaughs.com or www.kilkenny.ie

JUNE

Glastonbury Festival – Pilton, UK

Although it is always a bit of a nail-biter as to whether it will actually go ahead or not, the Glastonbury Festival seems to thrive on the 'where there's a will, there's a way' motto. Top bands on multiple stages perform in the festival, and controversy is the order of the day. Get grungy, get mullered, and always take your own loo roll. Check the website for the latest news on the state of play.
Web: www.glastonburyfestivals.co.uk

Roskilde Festival – Roskilde, Denmark

Europe's biggest and, reputedly, best rock music festival takes place at the end of June or beginning of July every year just outside Copenhagen. Profits are given to initiatives for youth projects or humanitarian work, and the event attracts major headline acts. In the past this has included traditional rock bands such as Metallica, Iron Maiden and Nirvana, along with Bob Marley and Coldplay. And you'll be surrounded by Scandinavian rock chicks.

Web: www.roskilde-festival.dk

JULY

Palio Horse Race – Siena, Italy

If you think the rivalry between Tottenham and Arsenal is fierce, you haven't seen the feuding districts of Palio go head to head in the annual horse race around the town's streets and squares. The rider who finishes first is hailed as a hero, anything less and a rider is branded the '98 Beckham of the district. Harsh. The flamboyant Italians spend a year planning the race and the result is a visual and culinary feast. The locals all recede to their district churches immediately after the race, but the celebrations go on way into the night.

Web: www.terresiena.it

S'Ardia Horse Race – Sardinia

Another frenetic horse race around a town's streets is held in Sardinia in the first week of July each year. It seems that in the absence of football in the summer months, the Italians need an alternative way to feed their passions. And that they certainly do. For up to three hours, a band of horsemen chase a single horseman around the town. No mean feat considering the searing heat of a Sardinian summer. And to keep the tension and excitement brewing, the spectators turn into a rabble, letting off guns, spaghetti western style, so be prepared to keep your distance. Go in cowboy-themed fancy dress and you could end up being national heroes.

Web: www.sarnow.com/sardinia/ardia1.htm

Wife-Carrying Championships – Sonkajärvi, Finland

An event highlight of the county fair in which participants race towards the finish line to win the equivalent of their wife's weight in beer. The rules are simple: the wife must be of a legal age and more than 49 kilos or she'll be weighed down accordingly. And there are extra prizes for the best costumes. Another event to watch out for is the beer-barrel-rolling contest. Participants are only allowed to use sticks to guide the barrel around a twisting course. How could a town with so much interest in beer fail to host an unforgettable stag do? The only drawback is that it's about 300 miles from Helsinki.

Web: www.sonkajarvi.fi

Running of the Bulls – Pamplona, Spain

Whether you go as a spectator or a participant, in which case organising a stag do is the least of your worries, this event will give you the perfect ice-breaker story to roll out for years to come. Everyone's heard of it, everyone's intrigued. The Fiesta of San Fermín runs from 6 to 14 July every year and is a non-stop whirl of partying, parades and bullfights. The daily running of the bulls (starting on 7 July) was originally just the way to transport them to the Plaza de Toros for the early evening fights. In recent years it's become more internationally renowned because of the runners who bait the bulls instead of herding them from behind. Plenty of people go just to watch and most runners are experienced, so unless you feel a particular need to put your life on the line, you don't necessarily have to participate to join in the fun. And be prepared – sleep deprivation is par for the course, with fireworks and partying every night and a marching band waking up the town between 6.30 and 7.00 every morning.

Web: www.pamplona.net

Witnness Festival – Dublin, Ireland

If you were looking for an excuse to head for Dublin, Witnness is fast becoming a highlight of the Irish music calendar. Every year, the Fairyhouse Racecourse plays host to some of the biggest name acts to appear in Ireland and the festival attracts the crowds you would expect. Stay for a day or the weekend and combine your trip with a night out in the city. To be sure.

Web: www.witnness.com

Schlagermove – Hamburg, Germany

A veritable feast of kitsch, this street festival pays homage to German retro-pop and 70s classics. 700,000 partygoers air their flares to turn out for this event every year, so it must be doing something right. A 70s porn star theme should ensure you fit right in.

Web: www.schlagermove.de

Love Parade – Berlin, Germany

If you are into dance music, this is the event for you as it is the biggest party of its kind and has an international reputation. Originally, the parade was predominantly a gay pride celebration similar to Mardi Gras in London, also in July. Now, it's a lot more diverse, attracting around half a million revellers every year for the festivities.

Web: www.loveparade.net

Burnin' Beatz – Cologne, Germany

Yes, it does have a dodgy name, courtesy of some enthusiastic translator no doubt. Billed as the biggest reggae, hip-hop and drum and base event in Europe, Burnin' Beatz takes place at the beginning of July. The setting is great, right on the banks of Lake Fuehlinger in the height of summer, with more than 200 performers. Go on, you know you've still got some body popping and swan dives left in you yet.

Web: www.burninbeatz.de (German language only)

Bastille Day – France

Embrace the ideals of *liberté*, *egalité* and *fraternité* with our French neighbours as they mark the anniversary of the storming of the Bastille on 13 and 14 July. The perfect excuse to combine your stag festivities with a trip to France. In Paris, every café, restaurant and club will be holding its own celebrations. Not to mention the endless partying in the streets, with a focus on the Champs Elysée, and the finale of a fantastic fireworks display at the Trocadéro. The Montmartre district is also renowned for walking on the wilder side and offers live strip shows.

Web: www.franceguide.com

Jazz Festival – Copenhagen, Denmark

Jazz along the canal banks. Jazz on the streets. Jazz in the cafés. With upwards of 600 performances spanning two weeks, this is a jazz lover's dream. And with the added bonus of a bounty of beautiful women to look at, what better location? Nice …

Web: www.jazzfestival.dk

Ollesummer – Tallinn, Estonia

The region's largest beer and music festival attracts crowds from all over the Nordic and Baltic countries, not forgetting local celebrities. Not that you'll recognise any of them, but the Estonians are welcoming and glad to see tourists enjoying themselves in their country. Plus you will be ahead of the crowd because this is the latest up-and-coming stag destination.

Web: www.ollesummer.ee

AUGUST

Notting Hill Carnival – London, UK

Depending on who you listen to, the Notting Hill Carnival is either the world's first or second largest street party with 2.5 million visitors and is held every August bank holiday weekend spanning the whole three days. In the daytime, a massive parade of elaborate floats, music, performers in fancy dress, and scantily clad women, snakes around the streets celebrating all the cultures that live in Britain today. At night, the partying really begins, with live bands on stages around Notting Hill and food stalls selling dishes from all over the world. It is fun, but not ideal for a large group as you'll find it difficult to stay together in the swarm of revellers.

Web: www.mynottinghill.co.uk/nottinghilltv/carnival-facts.htm

Race the Train – Tywyn, Wales

Yes, it is as bizarre as it sounds. Every year Tywyn, on the coast of North Wales, plays host to the 'Race the Train' event for anyone who feels the need to race a steam train over fifteen miles. If you've got a stag who is the energetic sort, then he shouldn't miss out. Except, he should have to take part in fancy dress, of course. That should cause a few blisters in interesting places. Once you are done racing the train, there are plenty more outdoorsy things to do in such a stunning part of the country, white-water rafting on the Treweryn being a favourite. Also look into hiring a castle or cottage to top off the lads' weekend.

Web: www.racethetrain.co.uk

Great Tomato Fight – Buñol, Spain

Why would people want to pelt the life out of each other with an arsenal of tomatoes? In order to find out, you need to go to The Great Tomato Fight (La Tomatina) that is held in Buñol every year to mark a historic food fight of yesteryear. The town's population is dwarfed by day visitors who come as enthusiastic participants to indulge in tomato war. The main sparring event lasts for just over an hour before the local fire department enters the affray to dowse everyone off, so a spare set of clothes is a wise move. Then everyone kicks back in high spirits in the local bars and restaurants to swap stories about their triumphs. Buñol is only a short train ride from Valencia, so you'll have the perfect opportunity to go back to the city for a great stag night out too.

Web: www.pilot.co.uk/festivals/tomatina.html

Bog Snorkelling Championships – Llanwrtyd Wells, Powys

They don't come much more alternative than this. Not ones to lie back while other nations dominate the world stage for strange and unusual events, Wales comes to the fore with this earthy number. Snorkellers must swim two lengths of a 50 metre murky trench cut into the peat. The fastest time wins a cash prize, which is billed as 'nominal' so watch out for the bits of pocket fluff included. Amazingly, competition is pretty stiff as the event attracts people from all over the world. Thank goodness it is in the name of charity.

Web: www.visitwales.com

Birdman Competition – Bognor Regis, UK

From its humble beginnings back in the early 1970s, the Bognor Birdman competition has gone from a sportsman's bet for a £3,000 prize to a hugely popular August bank holiday spectacle with a £25,000 prize. By all means, arrange for your stag to compete, but that will involve you building some kind of flying contraption before you get there. And, thankfully, in the 'Kingfisher class' judges are looking for humour rather than height or distance. Alternatively, sit in your deckchairs to laugh your heads off as wannabe flyers step up to the end of Bognor pier strapped to various devices only to crash and sink within seconds. In previous years, contestants have included Dumbo impersonators, bikes with mechanical wings attached, Pegasus, Icarus, and a man with a thousand balloons strapped to himself. And just so as you know, according to the website, 'catapults are not permitted'.

Web: www.birdman.org.uk

V2 Festival – Essex and Staffordshire, UK

Something in August that's not on the bank holiday weekend! Held the weekend before that, the V2 Festival is two-centred with one event in Chelmsford and another near Stafford. Bands quite often appear at both venues on different days. And this attracts the big acts too. Make a weekend out of it, or alternatively just go for the day and then arrange something else for a varied stag weekend.

Web: www.vfestival.com

Reading Festival – Reading, UK

Another 'must-do-before-I'm-30' music festival in our fair nation. Held over the August bank holiday, day or weekend tickets are available – so a tent and shovel aren't a pre-requisite if you don't want to stay overnight. Reading itself has had a regeneration programme running down by the waterfront so it's not bad for a night out. Alternatively, you're only 25 minutes from London on the express train or an hour from Bristol.

Web: www.readingfestival.com

Edinburgh Festival – Edinburgh, Scotland

Spanning the whole of August, the Edinburgh Festival runs concurrently with the Edinburgh Fringe and offers everything you would expect from the largest arts festival in the world. New and popular comic, musical and theatrical talent is here in abundance. The streets are alive with performers, every room big enough to swing a cat in it has a resident act, and the atmosphere is buzzing with excitement and expectation. Not to mention the ad hoc beer tents set up to cater to the enormous influx of visitors looking to moisten their palates throughout the day and night. For military gurus, the Edinburgh Military Tattoo takes place at the same time in the grounds of the castle but tickets for this are hard to come by and people book up way in advance to travel from all over the world.

Web: www.edfringe.com and www.eif.co.uk

Great British Beer Festival – Olympia, London

For beer lovers everywhere. Sample hundreds of kinds of beer, perry and scrumpy from the largest and smallest breweries, listen to live music and play the latest pub games. Just one word of caution: don't set your expectations too high because for a stag do it's essentially an excuse to get drunk in an exhibition hall, but it's a good daytime activity if you've got nothing else planned.

Web: www.gbbf.org

Mathew Street Festival – Liverpool, UK

Liverpool combines International Beatles Week (cue mop-top fancy dress theme) with the largest city centre music festival in the UK. Over 250,000 revellers roam the streets to watch bands performing on six stages around the city. Street performers are also out in force with one added bonus: the whole event is free.

Web: www.mathewstreetfestival.com

Creamfields – Liverpool, UK

One of the key dance events of the year, Creamfields brings together a host of talented DJs and bands the likes of Faithless and Underworld. Held at the old Liverpool Airport, it is getting bigger year on year. From just a dance event with a number of arenas, Creamfields now features fairground rides, a swimming pool and the legendary five-a-side football. Fun in the sun for one day only.

Web: www.cream.co.uk/creamfields

Homelands – Winchester, UK

Another one of the big old dance festivals that attracts the best acts, this time based in the south of England.

Web: www.homelands.co.uk

SEPTEMBER

Highland Games – Braemar, Scotland

Is your stag intent on getting married in a kilt, even though he's never even been to Scotland? In that case, as his best man, you need to give some strength to his convictions. Picture your stag tossing the caber, even though he would probably crumple under the sheer weight of it. The Highland Games are a chance to see what the Scots are made of, and the best games to visit are in Braemar. Surrounded by the most awesome scenery, watch events including tossing the caber and hammer, a tug-of-war, other strongman-type activities, and traditional Scottish entertainment with Highland dancers and pipers. At some of the Games, you can even have a go if you want. And if your group are outdoor types, you can also look into venturing into the wilderness for a night in the middle of nowhere. Amazing. Just make sure you get a ticket in advance to avoid disappointment.

Web: www.visitscotland.com

Oktoberfest - Munich, Germany

It might be September, but it's still time for Oktoberfest. Otherwise known as the beer festival, it is what Munich is best known for. A cacophony of boorish tourists, folk music, thigh slapping, beer swilling, fairground rides, shooting galleries, bands, parades and dancing engulfs the city for the

duration. Get your stag kitted out in lederhosen, give him a tankard for one hand and a sausage for the other, and try to pass him off as a local.
Web: www.oktoberfest.de

OCTOBER

Jeneverfeesten – Hasselt, Belgium

Other than chocolates, Belgium is known for its beer and waffles. What is not so well known is that it also has its own gin houses and, in October each year, the Belgians celebrate their hidden talents. For two days, the town of Hasselt revels in its produce and in recent years has even gone to the extent of having a free gin fountain. Pass the tonic.
Web: www.visitflanders.com

Goose Fair – Nottingham, UK

It's big. Very big. So if you're going to Nottingham at the beginning of October for your stag weekend and looking for something to do on the Friday night, then this could well do the trick. Thing is, it really is just a giant travelling fairground, albeit the largest in Europe, that's moved on somewhat from its thirteenth-century origins. Every year it attracts about half a million visitors. Of course, you can't go without sampling the local delicacy – mushy peas with mint sauce. Mmm?
Web: www.nottinghamgoosefair.co.uk

Italian Job Rally – UK to Italy

'You're only supposed to blow the bloody doors off!' Therein lie the immortal words of Sir Michael Caine. And you now have the chance to recreate your own stag *Italian Job*, using bottles of vino instead of gold bullion bars. Mini Coopers are the obvious choice, but the race organisers have relaxed the rules due to popular demand and now allow any car to take part as long as its model was featured in the original film. Vintage sports cars join the Minis and about 200 cars in total end up taking part in the 10-day rally from the UK through 2,500 miles and at least five countries to northern Italy. Once you arrive, there are several pre-arranged navigational rallies. Naturally these are *Italian Job*-style, through the narrow streets and countryside of the Emilia Romagna region, only stopping at vineyards on the way for more tasting and 'loot'. All a bit disorientating for the unsuspecting locals. And what makes it the more justifiable is that it is in the name of chariddy, mates. Stags on tour.

Web: www.italianjob.com

NOVEMBER

Berlin Jazz Festival – Berlin, Germany

More jazz. Nice. It seems that every city has its own jazz festival and November is the turn of Berlin. Since the end of the Cold War and fall of the Wall, the city has been reinventing itself to embrace and celebrate its diversity. If you need more convincing that it would be fun for a stag do, rest assured, Berlin has got a red light district too.

Web: www.berlinerfestspiele.de

Biggest Liar in the World Competition – Wasdale, Cumbria, UK

We are well past 'My dad's an astronaut' now. These whoppers would have got you a slap a few years ago. And perhaps if you're lucky they still might. Thanks to the proprietor of the Santon Bridge Inn, you can cheer yourselves up before descending into the bleak winter. Brighten up your November with the prospect of convincing judges that you are a natural born liar. Or just listen to the rest of the corkers that get told; pigs the size of cows, aliens, mermaids in the lakes, and chickens with two heads are all prolific in the area allegedly. And if the competition isn't enough to draw you to this neck of the woods, the stunning scenery around the Lake District should.

Web: www.santonbridgeinn.com/liar and www.golakes.co.uk

December

The Icehotel – Kiruna, Swedish Lapland

Every year, the Icehotel is re-designed and then re-built from the heavy snowfall in Lapland. Even when visitors are staying there, constant improvements are going on. From the hotel itself to a replica of Shakespeare's Globe, the buildings are magnificent and are adorned with ice sculptures. Furs are used to give warmth in the guest rooms. And then, every spring, the elaborate structures melt in the thaw to be built again the following year.

Web: www.artic-experience.co.uk and www.visit-sweden.com

The Cresta Run – St Moritz, Switzerland

From Christmas until March you are invited to take your chances on one of the fastest toboggan runs going. The treacherous bends and natural ice tracks throw racers from the course and the numerous casualties, including broken bones and even broken necks, bear testament to how dangerous this is. It is obvious that riders need extreme skill to negotiate the course, so why on earth they let complete novices on the track we have no idea. The organisers also say no block bookings. Perhaps due to the insurance companies' insistence? If you are interested in more information or would like to go as a spectator to enjoy rather than maim yourself, visit the official website.

Web: www.cresta-run.com

Varsity Match – Twickenham, UK

In its purest form, this is the annual challenge between Oxford and Cambridge first fifteens. But in order to turn it into an event, you need to start a bit earlier in the day. Kick-off is at The Fox and Anchor, EC1, with a cooked breakfast at 7 a.m. This is one of the pubs around Smithfield Market that has an early licence due to historic anomalies in the law putting the rights of market porters first. Moving through the city to Waterloo to get the train to Twickenham, this is the mother of all pub crawls. And then you get to top your day off with a trip to Richmond with everyone who's just starting on their drinking quest. Just follow the crowds.

Hogmanay – Edinburgh, Scotland

New Year's Eve with bells on. Hogmanay takes the celebration to new extremes with major bands playing on stages in the street, fireworks and a huge bonfire. And, as you'd expect, it is incredibly popular so advance bookings are a must, especially for a large group.

Web: www.edinburghshogmanay.org

Annual Sports Fixtures Calendar

If you've got a Sports Billy stag, think about going to a sporting day out. The major fixtures are listed below, with a couple from overseas thrown in for good measure. Double check dates as they can shift from year to year.

January

Ice Hockey – Super League Challenge Cup Final, London
(www.iceweb.co.uk)

February

Football – Scottish League Cup Final, Glasgow (www.scotprem.com)

Rugby Union – Six Nations: Paris, Dublin, Edinburgh, Twickenham, Cardiff, Rome (www.rfu.com)

Rugby Union – Celtic League Final, various Irish and Scottish venues (www.rfu.com)

Snooker – Masters Tournament, Wembley (www.worldsnooker.com)

March

Football – League Cup Final, Cardiff (www.thefa.com)

Horse Racing – Cheltenham National Hunt Festival and Gold Cup, Cheltenham (www.cheltenham.co.uk)

Horse Racing – Dubai World Cup, Dubai (www.dubaiworldcup.com)

Rugby Union – Six Nations: Paris, Dublin, Edinburgh, Twickenham, Cardiff, Rome (www.rfu.com)

April

Athletics – London Marathon, London (www.london-marathon.co.uk)

Horse Racing – Grand National, Aintree (www.aintree.co.uk/website/index.html)

Horse Racing – Irish Grand National, Fairyhouse (www.fairyhouseracecourse.ie)

Horse Racing – Scottish Grand National, Ayr (www.ayr-racecourse.co.uk)

Ice Hockey – Super League Play Off Finals, various UK rinks (www.iceweb.co.uk)

Rowing – Boat Race, London (www.theboatrace.org)

Rugby Union – English Cup Final, Twickenham (www.rfu.com)

Rugby League – Challenge Cup Final, Cardiff (www.rleague.com)

Snooker – World Championship, Sheffield (www.worldsnooker.com)

May

Football – FA Cup Final, Cardiff (www.thefa.com)

Football – Champions League Final, various European venues (www.uefa.com)

Motor Cycling – Isle of Man TT Festival, Isle of Man (www.ttwebsite.com)

Rugby Union – European Cup Final, various European venues (www.rfu.com)

Rugby Union – Shield Final, various European venues (www.rfu.com)

Rugby Union – Principality Cup Final, Cardiff (www.rfu.com)

Show jumping – Badminton Horse Trials (www.badminton-horse.co.uk)

Tennis – French Open, Paris (www.french.open-tennis.com)

June

Greyhound Racing – Greyhound Derby, Wimbledon (www.wimbledondogs.com)

Horse Racing – French Derby, Chantilly (www.france-galop.com)

Horse Racing – The Derby, Epsom (www.epsomderby.co.uk)

Horse Racing – Royal Ascot, Ascot (www.ascot.co.uk)

Motor Racing – Le Mans, Sarthe, France (www.lemans.org/2003/index.shtml)

Tennis – French Open, Paris (www.french.open-tennis.com)

Tennis – Queens Club tournament, London (www.queensclub.co.uk)

Tennis – Eastbourne, Nottingham and Bournemouth tournaments (www.lta.org.uk)

Tennis – The Championships, Wimbledon (www.wimbledon.org)

July

Cricket – Twenty-20 Semi-finals and final (www.ecb.co.uk)

Cycling – Tour de France, Rouen, France (www.letour.fr)

Formula One – British Grand Prix, Silverstone (www.bgp-f1.com)

Golf – British Open Championship, various UK and Ireland courses (www.opengolf.com)

Horse Racing – Glorious Goodwood, Goodwood (www.goodwood.co.uk)

Motor Cycling – British Grand Prix, Donington Park (www.donington-park.co.uk)

Motor Cycling – World Superbikes, Brands Hatch (www.worldsbk.com)

Rowing – Henley Royal Regatta, Henley (www.hrr.co.uk)

Tennis – The Championships, Wimbledon (www.wimbledon.org)

August

Athletics – British Grand Prix, Crystal Palace (www.ukathletics.net)

Cricket – England and Wales one-day final, Lord's (www.lords.org)

Horse Racing – Glorious Goodwood, Goodwood
(www.goodwood.co.uk)

Sailing – Cowes Week, Isle of Wight (www.cowesweek.co.uk)

September

Athletics – Great North Run, Newcastle (www.greatrun.org)

Gaelic Football – All Ireland Finals, Croke Park, Dublin (www.gaa.ie)

Horse Racing – St Leger, Doncaster (www.doncaster-racecourse.com)

Horse Racing – Irish St Leger, Curragh (www.curragh.ie)

Hurling – All Ireland Finals, Croke Park, Dublin (www.gaa.ie)

Tennis – US Open, New York (www.usopen.org)

October

Golf – World Match Play, Wentworth (www.wentworthclub.com)

Horse Racing – Prix de l'Arc de Triomphe, Longchamp, Paris
(www.france-galop.com)

Rugby League – Super League Grand Final, Manchester
(www.rleague.com)

November

Athletics – New York Marathon, New York, USA (www.nyrrc.org)

Motor Sport – World Rally Championship, various UK courses
(www.wrc.com)

December

Horse Racing – Boxing Day meeting, Kempton Park
(www.kempton.co.uk/website/index.html)

Fixtures Listings

For fixtures that run at various times throughout the year, check
out the following:

British Horse Racing Board (www.bhb.co.uk)

British Superbikes (www.british-superbikes.co.uk)

Cricket – Summer Test Series (www.ecb.co.uk)

Football Association – England and Wales
(www.thefa.com/www.premierleague.com)

Football – Scotland (www.scottishfa.co.uk)

Football – Ireland (www.fai.ie)

Grand Prix Formula One (www.fia.com or www.grandprix.com)

Rugby Football Union (www.rfu.com)

Over the Water Getaways

Any time is a good time to get online to find a cheapo flight away. Check out:

Berlin Air (www.airberlin.com)
BMI Baby (www.bmibaby.com)
easyJet (www.easyjet.com)
Fly.be (www.flybe.com)
MyTravelLite (www.mytravellite.com)
Ryanair (www.ryanair.com)
and Virgin Express (www.virginexpress.com) for deals.

Tourist information offices for the major destinations are listed here. Some of the more popular ones include Prague, Barcelona and Amsterdam, but check with the tourist information centre before booking to make sure stags haven't been caught drunk with their pants down once too often and been barred as a result.

Amsterdam

Tourist information: www.visitamsterdam.nl or
www.simplyamsterdam.nl

Stag appeal: Everyone knows about the red light district, sex museum, Banana Bar and Grasshopper pub, and for a normal red blooded male, that's enough. But in case you want to vary the pace there is always the possibility of an Ajax FC game, or a more cultural day taking a canal cruise.

Barcelona

Tourist information: www.barcelonaturisme.com or
www.simplygoingaround.com/barcelona

Stag appeal: Beaches, great Mediterranean atmosphere, a lively nightlife, sport and a fair dollop of culture for good measure. As home to Barcelona FC, Real Español FC, Barcelona Dragons (American Football) and a Formula One Grand Prix, it's also a sports Mecca. Get practising your flamenco and salsa moves to wow the señoritas.

Berlin

Tourist information: www.btm.de or
www.simplygoingaround.com/berlin

Stag appeal: Despite being a historic and cultural city, Berlin is still a crowd pleaser for stag parties with a red light district and Hertha Berlin

FC in residence. Its cutting-edge nightlife has a great reputation and the locals are heavily into their dance music. They also, bizarrely enough, have a name for themselves as great tango dancers.

Budapest

Tourist information: www.budapestinfo.hu

Stag appeal: This is a destination that is a bit out of the ordinary. Budapest offers saunas with the locals, Turkish baths and a Formula One Grand Prix, along with some lethal local brews to sting your stag with.

Copenhagen

Tourist information: www.woco.uk

Stag appeal: With a bounty of Scandinavian babes, a cracking night on the town with the light-hearted Danes is a winner, but apply for a bank loan before you leave home. And Christiania, the hippy district of the city, doesn't allow any photos but does have some interesting wares that are on sale by the slab so that they look like blocks of cheese. Copenhagen comes alive in summer with street performers, café culture and Tivoli Park, the city's amusement park. From Midsummer's Eve in June, the Danes put on endless summer music festivals with the highlight being Roskilde in June. In the winter, FC Copenhagen matches are an option for your sporting diary.

Dublin

Tourist information: www.visitdublin.com or
www.simplygoingaround.com/dublin

Stag appeal: If you are up for the *craic*, you need to head for Ireland for
home-grown Guinness, a relentless nightlife and Irish accents. If you're
planning to go in March, check for St Patrick's Day activities and book
early! Just one word to the wise: rumour has it that Dublin is putting
restrictions on stag parties trawling round Temple Bar, so check before
you book. Other sporting events to watch out for are six nations'
fixtures, horse racing at Fairyhouse, and hurling and Gaelic footie at
Croke Park.

Ibiza

Tourist information: www.ibiza-spotlight.com

Stag appeal: The clubbing haven in the sun, Ibiza has more to offer
than just its infamous nightlife. Great beaches, liberal sunbathing
attitudes, water sports and even a bit of sightseeing. The clubs are
pretty pricey so if you want to strike a balance between chilling and
partying, without ending up broke, stay on the quieter side of the
island. Top up that tan for the wedding!

Las Vegas

Tourist information: www.lasvegas.com

Stag appeal: Known for its mafia connections, shallow desert graves, gambling, excesses, plastic entertainers, big fights and proximity to the Grand Canyon, Las Vegas certainly has a colourful agenda to keep you amused. And for stag parties, there is the added attraction of the city's loose women and porn industry. Just don't get too drunk or you might end up marrying Elvis in the drive-thru chapel.

Madrid

Tourist information: www.aboutmadrid.com or
www.simplygoingaround.com/madrid

Stag appeal: The Spanish herald Madrid as the city that never sleeps. They've obviously forgotten about siestas then. Everything in the central district is accessible by foot and every street has small bars, cafés and tapas restaurants nestled in among the shops and houses. The main areas for going out are around the Plaza Major and Puerto del Sol, but you can also see Real Madrid FC and bullfighting a short metro ride away. The only drawbacks are that it is insanely hot in summer and it is not on the coast.

Munich

Tourist information: www.munich-tourist.de

Stag appeal: Time it right and don your lederhosen for the Oktoberfest beer festival. As Germany's second most popular tourist destination, there is plenty for visitors to do although a lot of it is perhaps a bit too cultural for a stag do. For the rest of the year, indulge in Munich's vibrant café culture, street performances and make the most of the varied nightlife. Plus there's pretty much guaranteed snow in the winter. For sports fans, you can take to the terraces for a Bayern Munich FC match.

New York

Tourist information: www.nyctourist.com or www.nycvisit.com

Stag appeal: The Big Apple has a unique buzz that will make your adrenaline rush and your wallet lighter. From seeing big-name acts perform at Madison Square Gardens to catching a Yankees or Giants game, to a night out in the Village or around Time Square, or even chilling out in Central Park, Manhattan has something for everyone. New Yorkers are known to be brash and big partygoers, so jump on their coat tails and hold on for the ride.

Paris

Tourist information: www.visit-paris.com or www.thingstodo-paris.com

Stag appeal: The city of romance can also show a stag and his bucks a good time. This is, after all, the country that serves beer in a Disney park, and the French drink wine with everything and at any time of day. As with any other capital city, Paris has lots going on all year round, so check for the latest events calendars on the web. And Montmartre offers up Paris's equivalent of a red light district. For travel, although there are cheap airlines, Eurostar is a great option that even offers a 'night clubber fare' if you don't want to fork out for a hotel. See www.eurostar.com for details.

Prague

Tourist information: www.praguetourist.com or www.visitprague.cz

Stag appeal: Medieval and gothic architecture frames this striking city on the river Vltava. Since it kicked the hand of Communism into touch, Prague has been eagerly chasing the capitalist dream, while still trying to hold on to its culture and heritage. A favourite with stag parties for a while now, the locals aren't quite as enamoured with groups of lads 'just having their fun' as they used to be, but you will still have a great time all the same. The Czech Republic is also the home of the original Pilsner lager. Medieval banquets, live music, beer Kellers, beautiful women and cheap, quality booze await.

Reykjavik

Tourist information: www.tourist.reykjavik.is or www.reykjavik.com

Stag appeal: Everything is more expensive than in the UK and yet Reykjavik is one of the most popular non-budget destinations for Brits. Once you have been it's clear to see why – the city is surrounded by breathtaking scenery, has an ultra cool nightlife and world-renowned thermal spas to relax your stag before the big day. Scientists are also investigating the healing properties of Icelandic volcanic dust for various ailments, with hangovers at the top of the hit list. A bit of interesting local trivia – the oldest pub in the city opened before full-strength beer was legalised; the locals had to wait until 1989 for their first quality tipple. Investigate what is going on before you book. Remember that in the height of the tourist season in summer, Reykjavik has a midnight sun, which means there is no night, whereas in the depths of winter there are only two hours of half-light in an otherwise dark day. The Northern Lights (or Aurora Borealis) are visible from September to October and February to March.

Stockholm

Tourist information: www.stockholmtown.com

Stag appeal: Pricey beer but with enough eye candy to make you fat, who cares? Stockholm is another charming and cultural Scandinavian city permeated by waterways, but with more of a cosmopolitan flavour than most. As Sweden's capital it has all the activities, amenities and nightlife options you would expect, but at three times the price of everywhere else it could be a steep budget to expect everyone to stump up.

Tallinn

Tourist information: www.tallinn.ee

Stag appeal: Fancy shooting off a few rounds from an old Kalashnikov rifle, tank driving or jet flying? Then this is the place for you. Thanks to the end of the Cold War and Russia being bankrupted, your dreams can come true. Estonia is reasonably priced for a country bordering Scandinavia, although not as cheap as you would expect. It is a summer destination because in winter the icy conditions mean everything stops. Watch out for the nation's largest music festival, Ollesummer, held every July … If you still think Prague is the latest stag hotspot – then it's time you took a look at Tallinn.

Warsaw

Tourist information: www.warsaw-travel.com or www.warsaw1.net

Stag appeal: The Polish capital has not developed the wild and plentiful nightlife that might be the order of the day for some stag dos. But if you are looking for a more cultural and calmer weekend away that involves a less demanding drinking and clubbing element, then consider visiting this stunning city. Definitely alternative.

Shop in Seconds

Props for the forfeits. Treats for the bucks or stag. Whatever it is that you are after, try these places for some novel ideas.

The Gadget Shop: From battery-operated claptrap to novelty games, gadgets and fluffy handcuffs, this is a great place for inspiration.

Firebox: Big boys' toys and gadgets. Firebox is more appropriate for a keepsake present. See www.firebox.com.

Ann Summers: From the ridiculous to the sublime. Britain does high-street raunch. Good for props for the stag night.

Claire's Accessories, H&M (Hennes) and New Look:

Yes, these are women's shops. And they're the cheapest you're going to get – ideal for the stag in drag. Now all you've got to do is convince the sales assistant that you're shopping for your XXL-sized sister.

Finishing Touches

So, you have planned a brilliant stag night that your mates will rave about for years to come. But have you got all the little things covered? Here are a few options for you to consider.

A 'fines' lucky dip bag

Take miniatures in a bag so that you can dish them out as drinking penalties over the weekend, for example, for being late. The offender must go for a lucky dip and take his chances.

Point man

Assign different point men throughout the evening. Their sole purpose is to round up girls to come and talk to you or 'entertain' you.

Challenge cards

If you're planning on giving your stag challenges while he's out, consider making them up in advance so that it is a bit more compelling for him to do them. You might even want to tie the look of the cards in with the theme, or use this as an opportunity to incorporate the compromising photos you've got of the stag from over the years.

Shirt swapping – not lifting

If you're not going the whole hog and are avoiding the fancy dress themes, you will need to have something else to make the night a bit different. This idea might just save your night, although if the bucks don't know each other, it could be interesting trying to convince them that they want to do it. Shirt swapping. Every half hour. Throughout the night. Regardless of location, whether that be on a packed train, bus full of shoppers, toilet, bar or restaurant. Set up an order that means a buck always takes a shirt from the same buck, and gives his shirt to the same other buck. If a player misses out or takes too long, there's a four-finger drinking fine.

Limos

Hire a limo to get the stag party to the night out in style. Everyone's a limo lush at heart so use this as an excuse to push the … er … car out. You can even hire lap-dancing limo services, although check out their websites first to see what you are letting yourselves in for.

Cigars

Need we say more?

Forfeits by the bucks

As an alternative to preparing the challenges in advance, at the start of the night get all the bucks to write a forfeit on a bit of card. The twist is that during the evening, each buck has to take their turn to pull a card out of the hat and then they must also do the forfeit with the stag. Woe betide anyone who gets malicious in their creativity, only to pull out their own challenge.

Scavenger hunt

Prepare a scavenger list for your stag before the big night. Be sure to include one item of women's underwear, a tampon, a free drink from a barmaid, and a single free fish finger.

Wigs

Suffice it to say, never underestimate the power of the wig.

Disposable cameras

To catch it on film, or not catch it on film? That is the question. The beauty of a disposable camera is that it doesn't matter if it gets lost, and you can also destroy the evidence without girlfriends or wives being any the wiser.

Hangover Hard Hitters

The reality is that you've got a hangover because you've poisoned your body by drinking enough alcohol to keep a pub afloat for a week. These might help get you to the point where you can move without needing to throw up. From the sublime to the ridiculous ...

Bedside help

Before you go out, prepare for the worst. The reason you feel so terrible the morning after the night before is because your body is protesting at being deficient in sugar and water, which your liver has used up while fighting the good fight. So help yourself out by having a large sugary, water-based drink before you go to sleep and when you wake up. Caffeine is also a toxin, so it's best to avoid that. And don't take painkillers before you go to sleep because, contrary to popular belief, they can irritate your stomach and liver further – you might find you're worse off, if not immediately, then longer term.

Cholesterol cure

Theories abound about the types of chemicals and components in a hearty English fry-up and what they do. Everyone knows it's not healthy, but it is traditional, the lion's share is 'natural' and, most importantly, it does seem to work. Give your body some energy to get you back on track, and boost your mineral intake with a sprinkling of salt.

Peppermint and ginger

Who knows what you're willing to try? Especially in front of the lads. But peppermint is renowned to be good for digestion and ginger is a natural remedy for nausea. So ditch the English breakfast tea and opt for the herbals instead if you know what's good for you.

Hair of the dog

This originates from Roman times as 'take the hair of the dog that bit you'. They believed that if a rabid dog bit you, a concoction including a hair of that dog could cure you. Questionable. With regard to hangovers, as you have probably guessed, all this does is suspend the inevitable, and give your liver the equivalent of a second going over.

Vitamin C

It seems as if people pop vitamin C tablets every time they feel a bit run down. And if you think of a hangover in terms of being run down, rather than being toxically bruised, then the same applies. Good natural sources are oranges and tomatoes. Or lemons and limes if you're able to eat those without wincing. Alternatively, pop down the shops for some tonic or effervescent tablets.

Serpentine Swimming Club

Fancy a dip? Because every Saturday at 8 a.m., a group of enthusiastic Londoners gather at the Serpentine in Hyde Park for a swim in the lake. Whatever the weather. They brave it in the depths of winter and the polluted highs of summer. It should definitely shock your system into doing something anyway. See:
www.serpentineswimmingclub.com/index.htm.

To Do Checklist

Three months before

- [ ] Check with the stag if he's got a dying wish to go somewhere specific.
- [ ] Get a list of prospective bucks from the stag, with a heads up as to likely budgets and availability.
- [ ] See the sporting fixtures and events sections for ideal activities to suit your group.
- [ ] Give the bucks two possible weekends to block out so you have the flexibility to scout around for the best deals and activities.
- [ ] Book accommodation for everyone and be sure to get a booking reference. You may need to book this further in advance if your weekend is during peak season or while special events are on.

Two months before

- [ ] Choose your theme (and aim to keep it as a surprise for your stag).
- [ ] Book your transport if you are not driving, to take advantage of advance fare offers.

One month before

☐ Check if the bucks are happy to have a kitty for getting the extras for the weekend.

☐ Start planning and co-ordinating your outfits and props for the theme.

☐ Start planning what you are going to have to get for the stag for the theme.

☐ Book your daytime and Friday night activities and be sure to get a booking reference (you may need to do this further in advance if you have a large group or if it is something that will get booked up).

☐ Book restaurants if you are planning on eating out, especially if you are a large group. And, again, make sure you get a booking reference.

Two weeks before

☐ Check if you can get on the guest list at your chosen nightclub to save queuing. Unlikely, but it can't hurt.

One week before

☐ Confirm your accommodation and activity bookings.

☐ Make sure you have everything you need for the theme covered, for you and the stag.

☐ Prepare the challenge cards.

The day before

☐ Confirm that everyone knows where and when to meet.

☐ Let everyone know if they owe you any money so far so that they are prepared.

☐ Buy enough camera film or disposable cameras to last the night or weekend.

☐ Stock up on any hangover cures that you will need for the morning after.

☐ Confirm any restaurant reservations.

The 'do' itself

☐ Check you have got your camera, kitty, challenge cards and props ready and to hand.

☐ Take a record of any reference numbers or names you have been given as confirmation of bookings in case you have any problems when you get to venues.

☐ Get a kitty together to pay for rounds of drinks and the meal – this will save any hassle with splitting the bill.

Shags and Hags

If your stag has made it to 30 without getting hitched, he is more likely to have a shag or a hag. Fear not, it's not as bad as it sounds …

From the stag's point of view, he's blown it too many times in the past to risk it now. Not to mention the fact that his mum will kill him if he screws this one up. He has also realised that his fiancée is his best mate and he would rather have a night that includes her and their shared mates than another lagered-up, lechy stag do with nightmarish mates he is never going to see again. It happens.

If this is the case then the themes, games and activities in this book still stand. There's also an *Alternative Hen* book, which might help to find the right middle ground for a 'shag'. Just bear in mind that you will have to compromise the kind of activities you get up to – don't get the stag and hen to carry out the more flirtatious challenges if it's likely to end up in a bar brawl.

Top activities in the directory suited to mixed groups are:

- ◆ canal boats;
- ◆ castle or cottage;
- ◆ circus school;
- ◆ clay pigeon shooting;
- ◆ It's a Knockout;
- ◆ karting;
- ◆ outdoor activity centres;
- ◆ white-water rafting.

Stag Do in a Box

Finally, if you just don't have the time or the inclination to plan your festivities, let someone do it for you. These companies will take it all out of your hands:

Chilli Sauce
Telephone: 0845 450 7450
Web: www.chillisauce.co.uk

Crocodile Events
Telephone: 0115 911 5758
Web: www.crocodileevents.co.uk

Eclipse Leisure
Telephone: 0870 2000 6969
Web: www.eclipseleisure.com

Great Escapades
Telephone: 0870 010 0505
Web: www.great-escapades.org

Great Weekends
Telephone: 0845 450 4333
Web: www.great-weekends.co.uk

Last Night of Freedom
Telephone: 0870 751 4433
Web: www.lastnightoffreedom.co.uk

Organize Events
Telephone: 0845 330 3940
Web: www.organize-events.co.uk

Playaway Weekends
Telephone: 01225 350 075
Web: www.playawayweekends.com

Red Seven Leisure
Telephone: 0870 751 7377
Web: www.stagparty.co.uk

Suggested Accommodation

Hotel chains are good for booking accommodation for groups but if you fancy something a bit more personal contact the local tourist information centre for a list of options.

Best Western
Telephone: 08457 747474
Web: www.bestwestern.co.uk

De Vere Hotels
Telephone: 0870 606 3606
Web: www.devereonline.co.uk

Holiday Inn
Telephone: 0870 400 8161
Web: www.holidayinn.co.uk

Thistle Hotels
Telephone: 0870 333 9292
Web: www.thistlehotels.co.uk

Travel Inn
Telephone: 0870 242 8000
Web: www.travelinn.co.uk

Travel Lodge
Telephone: 08700 850950
Web: www.travelodge.co.uk

Alternative Directory

This directory will give you a starting point for activities in a selection of cities around the UK. They are listed in alphabetical order and will help you to plan where to go and what to do for your Alternative Stag night.

Listings under Outdoor Activity Centres include: 4 x 4 driving, abseiling, archery, blindfold driving, canyoning, caving, clay pigeon shooting, climbing, gorge walking, Honda pilots, hovercraft, It's a Knockout, quad biking, raft racing, ropes courses.

Under Watersports (and some Outdoor Activity Centres) you will find: canoeing, jet-skiing, kayaking, powerboating, sailing, surfing, wakeboarding, waterskiing, windsurfing.

Avoid disappointment

When you are choosing which nightclub to go to, it goes without saying that you will need to check whether there is a dress code. And it's worth trying to get on the guest list so you don't have to queue.

And be sure to have a look at the 'More Alternative Activities' section at the end for even more unique ideas.

This isn't a watertight list and you should make sure that the listing you choose fits the style and budget you're after. If you can't find what you are looking for then call up the local tourist information centre or have a browse around the Internet.

BATH

Bath Tourist Information Centre
Abbey Chambers, Abbey Church Yard
Bath BA1 1LY
Telephone: 0906 711 2000
Email: tourism@bathnes.gov.uk
Web: www.visitbath.co.uk or www.bath.info

Comedy Clubs
See Bristol listings.

Flying
Bath, Wilts & North Dorset Gliding Club
The Park, Kingston Deverill, Warminster BA12 7HS
Telephone: 01985 844095
Web: www.bwnd.co.uk

Golf
Bath Approach Golf Course (pitch & putt)
Victoria Park, Bath BA1 2NR
Telephone: 01225 331162
Web: www.bathpublicgolf.co.uk

Entry Hill Golf Club
Entry Hill, Bath BA2 5NA
Telephone: 01225 834248
Web: www.bathpublicgolf.co.uk

Combe Grove Manor Driving Range
Brassknocker Hill, Monkton Combe
Bath BA15 7HS
Telephone: 01225 835533
Web: www.combegrovemanor.com

Horse Racing
Bath Racecourse
Lansdown, Bath BA1 9BU
Telephone: 01225 424609
Web: www.bath-racecourse.co.uk

Horse Riding
See High Action under Outdoor Activity Centres
for Bristol.

Hot Air Ballooning
Balloons Over Bath
Greenacre Lodge, Breadstone, Berkeley GL13 9HF
Telephone: 01453 810018
Web: www.balloonsoverbath.co.uk

Bath Balloon Flights
8 Lambridge, London Road, Bath BA1 6BJ
Telephone: 01225 466888
Web: www.balnet.co.uk

First Flight (Central Bath)
Telephone: 01225 484060
Web: www.firstflight.co.uk

Karting
Castle Combe Kart Track
Castle Combe Circuit, Chippenham SN14 7EX
Telephone: 01249 783010
Web: www.combe-events.co.uk

Nightclubs
Cadillacs
90B Walcot Street, Bath BA1 5BG
Telephone: 01225 464241

Babylon
Kingston Road, Bath BA1 1PQ
Telephone: 01225 400404
Web: www.ponana.co.uk

Outdoor Activity Centres
Pursuits
33 Reybridge, Lacock, Chippenham SN15 2PF
Telephone: 01249 730388
Activities: archery, blindfold driving, clay pigeon
shooting, quad biking

Mill On The Brue
Trendle Farm, Bruton BA10 0BA
Telephone: 01749 812307
Web: www.millonthebrue.co.uk
Activities: abseiling, archery, canoeing, clay pigeon
shooting, climbing, grass skiing, grass toboggans,
jet skiing, quad biking, raft racing, zip wire

Combe Grove Manor Hotel & Country Club
Brassknocker Hill, Monkton Combe
Bath BA15 7HS
Telephone: 01225 835533
Web: www.combegrovemanor.com
Activities: archery, casino evenings, clay pigeon
shooting, It's a Knockout, murder mystery, quad
biking, reverse steer car races, themed barge nights

See also High Action under Outdoor Activity
Centres for Bristol

Paintball
See Bristol listings.

Scuba Diving
Bath Dive Centre
Upper Bristol Road, 1 Cork Place, Bath BA1 3BB
Telephone: 01225 482081
Web: www.bathdivecentre.co.uk

Skiing & Snowboarding
See High Action under Outdoor Activity Centres
for Bristol.

Table-side Dancing Clubs
See Bristol listing.

Watersports
Cotswold Water Park
Keynes Country Park, Shorncote
Cirencester GL7 6DF
Telephone: 01285 861459
Web: www.waterpark.org

BELFAST

Belfast Welcome Centre
47 Donegall Place, Belfast BT1 5AD
Telephone: 02890 246609
Email: belfastwelcomecentre@nitic.net
Web: www.gotobelfast.com

Flying
Ulster Flying Club
Ards Airport, Portaferry Road
Newtownards BT23 8SG
Telephone: 02891 813327
Web: www.ulsterflyingclub.com

Golf
Mount Ober Driving Range
24 Ballymaconaghy Road, Knockbracken BT8 6SB
Telephone: 02890 795666

Craigavon Golf Centre
Turmoya Lane, Silverwood, Lurgan BT66 6NG
Telephone: 02838 326606
Web: www.craigavonboroughcouncil.gov.uk

Horse Racing
Down Royal Racecourse
Maze, Lisburn BT27 5RW
Telephone: 02892 621256
Web: www.downroyal.com

Horse Riding
Lagan Valley Equestrian Centre
170 Upper Malone Rd, Dunmurry
Belfast BT17 9JZ
Telephone: 02890 614853

Karting
Formula Karting
Greenbank Business Centre
Warrenpoint Road, Newry BT34 2QX
Telephone: 02830 266220
Web: www.formula-karting.com

Ultimate Karting
11 Kilbride Road, Doagh, Ballyclare BT39 0QA
Telephone: 02893 342777
Web: www.ultimatekarting.com

Nightclubs
Benedicts
7–21 Bradbury Place, Belfast BT7 1RQ
Telephone: 02890 591999
Web: www.benedictshotel.co.uk

Robinsons
38–42 Great Victoria Street, Belfast BT2 7BA
Telephone: 02890 247447
Web: www.belfastpubs-n-clubs.com

Empire Bar
42 Botanic Avenue, Belfast BT7 1JQ
Telephone: 02890 249276
Web: www.belfastpubs-n-clubs.com

Outdoor Activity Centres
Corporate Solutions
Lower Knockbarragh Road, Rostrevor BT34 3DP
Telephone: 02841 739333
Web: www.eastcoastadventure.com or
www.corporate.ie
Activities: abseiling, banana skiing, clay pigeon
shooting, deep sea fishing, golf, helicopter flights,
horse riding, jet skiing, powerboats, rock climbing,
yachting

Protosport
61 Mullantine Road, Portadown BT62 4EJ
Telephone: 02838 331919
Web: www.protosport.co.uk
Activities: karting, off-road buggies, quad biking

Paintball
Escarmouche Paintball
Unit 5, 19 Donegall Pass, Belfast BT7 1DR
Telephone: 02890 327500
Web: www.escarmouche.com

Scuba Diving
Blue Juice Diving
Telephone: 02886 735881
Web: www.bluejuicediving.com
Activities: scuba diving, mountain biking, archery,
paragliding

Skiing & Snowboarding
Craigavon Ski and Golf Centre
Turmoya Lane, Silverwood, Lurgan BT66 6NG
Telephone: 02838 326606
Web: www.craigavonboroughcouncil.gov.uk

Table-side Dancing Clubs
Movie Star Café
(lap dancing restaurant for men and women)
69 Botanic Ave, Belfast BT7 1JL
Telephone: 02890 238643

Tenpin Bowling
Belfast Superbowl
4 Clarence Street West, Bedford Street
Belfast BT2 7GP
Telephone: 02890 331466

The Dogs
Ballyskeagh Greyhound Stadium
New Grosvenor Park, Ballyskeagh Road
Lambeg BT17 9LL
Telephone: 02890 616720

Watersports
Lagan Watersports Centre
2 Rivers Edge, 13–15 Ravenhill Road
Belfast BT6 8DN
Telephone: 02890 461711
Web: www.laganwatersports.co.uk
Activities: canoeing, dragon boating, kayaking,
power boating, rowing, sailing

Craigavon Watersports Centre
1 Lake Road, Craigavon BT64 1AS
Telephone: 02838 342669
Activities: banana boating, canoeing, dragon
boating, kayaking, sailing, wake boarding, water
skiing, windsurfing

BIRMINGHAM

Tourist Information Centre
2 City Arcade, Birmingham B2 4TX
Telephone: 0121 202 5099
Web: www.beinbirmingham.com or
www.marketingbirmingham.com

Casinos
Grosvenor Casino
263 Broad Street, Birmingham B1 2HF
Telephone: 0121 631 3535
Web: www.rank.com

Gala Casino
Hill Street, Birmingham B5 4AH
Telephone: 0121 643 1777
Web: www.galacasinos.co.uk

Comedy Clubs
Jongleurs
Quayside Tower, 259/262 Broad Street
Birmingham B1 2HF
Telephone: 0870 240 5721
Web: www.jongleurs.co.uk

Flying
Avon Flying School
Wellesbourne-Mountford Airfield
Wellesbourne CV35 9EU
Telephone: 01789 470727
Web: www.avonflyingschool.com

Flightworks (Midlands) Ltd
Rowley Road, Coventry CV3 4FR
Telephone: 02476 511100
Web: www.flightworks.co.uk

Golf
Cocks Moors Woods Golf Course
Alcester Road South, Kings Heath B14 4ER
Telephone: 0121 464 3584
Web: www.birmingham.gov.uk

Hilltop Golf Course
Park Lane, Handsworth B21 8LJ
Telephone: 0121 554 4463
Web: www.birmingham.gov.uk

Hatchford Brook Golf Centre
Coventry Road, Sheldon B26 3PY
Telephone: 0121 743 9821
Web: www.birmingham.gov.uk

Horse Racing
Warwick Racecourse
Hampton Street, Warwick CV34 6HN
Telephone: 01926 491553
Web: www.warwickracecourse.co.uk

Horse Riding
Hole Farm Trekking Centre
Woodgate Valley Country Park
36 Watery Lane, Quinton B32 3BS
Telephone: 0121 422 3464

Cottage Farm Riding Stables
100 Ilshaw Heath Rd
Warings Green, Hockley Heath B94 6DL
Telephone: 01564 703314

Hot Air Ballooning
Balloons Over The Midlands
Greenacre Lodge, Breadstone, Berkeley GL13 9HF
Telephone: 01453 810018
Web: www.balloonsoverthemidlands.co.uk

Indoor Activity Centres
The Birmingham Indoor Climbing Centre,
The Rockface
A.B. Row, Off Jennens Road
Millennium Point, Birmingham B4 7QT
Telephone: 0121 359 6419
Web: www.rockface.co.uk
Activities: abseiling, caving, climbing, blind wine-
tasting, rope bridges and other challenges

Karting
Grand Prix Karting
Birmingham Wheels Park, Adderley Road South
Birmingham B8 1AD
Telephone: 0121 327 7617
Web: www.grandprixkarting.co.uk

Nightclubs
Brannigans
200–209 Broad Street, Birmingham B15 1AY
Telephone: 0121 616 1888

Zanzibar
Hurst Street, Birmingham B5 4AS
Telephone: 0121 643 4715
Web: www.zanzibar.co.uk

Tiger Tiger
Five Ways, Broad Street, Birmingham B15 1AY
Telephone: 0121 643 9722
Web: www.tigertiger.co.uk

Outdoor Activity Centres
The Ackers
Golden Hillock Road, Sparkbook B11 2PY
Telephone: 0121 772 5111
Web: www.theackers.co.uk
Activities: abseiling, archery, bowboats, canoeing,
climbing, kayaking, orienteering, skiing,
snowboarding

Wolverhampton Clay Target Club
The Cooking House, Himley, Dudley
Telephone: 01902 790992
Web: www.lesplantshooting.co.uk
Activities: clay pigeon shooting

Paintball
National Paintball Fields (Bassetts Pole)
Metro Triangle, Mount Street, Nechells B7 5QT
Telephone: 0800 358 3959
Web: www.nationalpaintballfields.com

SAS Paintball
Woodhall Farm, Wood Road
Codsall Wood WV8 1QS
Telephone: 01902 844467
Web: www.saspaintball.com

Scuba Diving
Scuba Sport
15 Whitminster Avenue, Birmingham B24 9NG
Telephone: 0121 384 5595
Web: www.scubasport.co.uk

Skiing & Snowboarding
The Snowdome
Leisure Island, River Drive, Tamworth
Staffordshire B79 7ND
Telephone: 0870 500 0011
Web: www.snowdome.co.uk

Also see The Ackers under Outdoor Activity
Centres

Table-side Dancing Clubs
Spearmint Rhino
64 Hagley Road, Birmingham B16 8PF
Telephone: 0121 455 7656
Web: www.spearmintrhino.com

Spearmint Rhino Extreme
John Bright Street, Birmingham B1 1BN
Telephone: 0121 633 7456
Web: www.spearmintrhino.com

Tenpin Bowling
Megabowl
Pershore Street, Birmingham B5 4RW
Telephone: 0121 666 7525
Web: www.megabowl.co.uk

The Dogs
Hall Green Track
York Road, Hall Green B28 8LQ
Telephone: 0870 840 7400
Web: www.hallgreenstadium.co.uk

Watersports
Hydro Extreme
Action Sports Centre, Worcester Road, Holt
Worcester WR6 6NH
Telephone: 01905 620044
Web: www.hydroextreme.com

H20 Sports
202 Saltwells Road, Dudley DY2 0BL
Telephone: 01384 633984
Web: www.h2osports.co.uk

BLACKPOOL

Tourist Information Centre
1 Clifton Street, Blackpool FY1 1LY
Telephone: 01253 478222
Email: tourism@blackpool.gov.uk
Web: www.blackpooltourism.com

Casinos
Grosvenor Casino
Sandcastle, South Promenade, Blackpool FY4 1BB
Telephone: 01253 341222
Web: www.rank.com

Flying
Blackpool Pleasure Flights
Blackpool Air Centre, Blackpool Airport FY4 2QS
Telephone: 01253 341871

Golf
Stanley Park Municipal Golf Course
Telephone: 01253 395349
Web: www.blackpool.gov.uk

Horse Racing
Haydock Park Racecourse
Newton-Le-Willows WA12 0HQ
Telephone: 01942 402624
Web: www.haydock-park.com

Hot Air Ballooing
Balloons Over Blackburn
Greenacre Lodge, Breadstone, Berkeley GL13 9HF
Telephone: 01453 810018
Web: www.balloonsoverblackburn.co.uk

Karting
Karting 2000
New South Promenade, Blackpool FY4 1TB
Telephone: 01253 406340
Web: www.karting2000.com

Kapitol Karting
275–289 Central Drive, Blackpool FY1 5HZ
Telephone: 01253 292600
Web: www.kapitolkarting.co.uk

Nightclubs
The Syndicate
Church Street, Blackpool FY1 3PR
Telephone: 01253 753222
Web: www.thesyndicate.org

The Waterfront
168–170 North Promenade, Blackpool FY1 1RE
Telephone: 01253 292900
Web: www.ukcn.com

Heaven and Hell
Bank Hey Street, Blackpool FY1 4QZ
Telephone: 01253 625118
Web: www.heavenandhell.co.uk

Outdoor Activity Centres
Adrenalin Zone
South Pier, Promenade, Blackpool FY4 1BB
Telephone: 01253 292029
Web: www.blackpoollive.com
Activities: reverse bungee jump, roller-coasters

Adventure 21
21 Babylon Lane, Anderton, Chorley PR6 9NR
Telephone: 01257 474467
Web: www.adventure21.co.uk
Activities: aquaseiling, abseiling, canoeing, caving,
canyoning, climbing, culvert scrambling, gorge
scrambling, kayaking, mountain biking,
orienteering, raft building, windsurfing

A6 Clay Target Centre
Reeves House Farm, Fourgates
Westhoughton, Bolton BL5 3LY
Telephone: 01942 843578
Web: www.a6ctc.co.uk
Activities: clay pigeon shooting

Paintball
Sudden Impact Paintball
Whyndyke Farm, Preston New Road
Blackpool FY4 4XQ
Telephone: 01253 313163
Web: www.sudden-impact.co.uk

Table-side Dancing Clubs
Sinless
111–115 Central Promenade, Blackpool FY1 5BD
Telephone: 01253 621888
Web: www.sinless.co.uk

Tenpin Bowling
Premier Bowl
Mecca Buildings, Central Drive, Blackpool FY1 5HZ
Telephone: 01253 295503
Web: www.premierbowlblackpool.com

BOURNEMOUTH

The Visitor Information Bureau
Westover Road, Bournemouth BH1 2BU
Telephone: 0906 802 0234 (calls charged at 60p
per minute)
Email: info@bournemouth.gov.uk
Web: www.bournemouth.co.uk

Casinos
Gala Casinos
Westover Road, Bournemouth BH1 2BZ
Telephone: 01202 553790
Web: www.galacasinos.co.uk

Comedy Clubs
Check with the Visitor Information Bureau for
comedy nights.

Flying
Bournemouth Flying Club
Aviation Park East, Off Matchams Lane
Bournemouth International Airport
Christchurch BH23 6NE
Telephone: 01202 578558
Web: www.bournemouthflyingclub.co.uk

Flying Frenzy Paragliding
1 Mill Terrace, Burton Bradstock
Bridport DT6 4QY
Telephone: 01308 897909
Web: www.flyingfrenzy.com

Golf

Meyrick Park Golf Course
Central Drive, Bournemouth BH2 6LH
Telephone: 01202 786040
Web: www.clubhaus.com

Horse Racing

The Bibury Club Ltd
Salisbury Racecourse, Netherhampton
Salisbury SP2 8PN
Telephone: 01722 326461
Web: www.salisburyracecourse.co.uk

Horse Riding

Sandford Park Riding Stables
Sandford Holiday Park, Holton Heath
Poole BH16 6JZ
Telephone: 01202 621782

Hot Air Ballooning

British School of Ballooning
Little London, Ebernoe, Nr Petworth GU28 9LF
Telephone: 01428 707307
Web: www.hotair.co.uk

Balloons Over Dorset
Greenacre Lodge, Breadstone, Berkeley GL13 9HF
Telephone: 01453 810018
Web: www.balloonsoverdorset.co.uk

Karting

Southern Counties Karting
Wardon Hill, Nr Dorchester DT2 9PW
Telephone: 01935 83666
Web: www.southern-counties.com

Nightclubs

Jumpin Jaks
The Waterfront, Pier Approach
Bournemouth BH2 5AA
Telephone: 07000 311311
Web: www.jumpinjaks.co.uk

Bar Med
The Quadrant Centre
St Peter's Road, Bournemouth BH1 2AB
Telephone: 01202 299537
Web: www.bar-med.com

Outdoor Activity Centres

Henley Hillbillies
Old Henley Farm, Buckland Newton
Dorchester DT2 7BL
Telephone: 01300 345293
Web: www.henleyhillbillies.co.uk
Activities: archery, clay pigeon shooting,
crossbows, hovercraft, mini mavriks, quad biking

Brenscombe Outdoor Centre
Studland Road, Corfe Castle, Dorset BH20 5JG
Telephone: 01929 481222
Web: www.brenscombeoutdoor.co.uk
Activities: abseiling, archery, canoeing, climbing,
horseriding, kayaking, laser clay shooting,
mountain biking, powerboating, quad biking, raft
building, ropes course, survival skills, waterskiing,
windsurfing

Matchams Leisure Park
Hurne Road, Matchams, Nr Ringwood BH24 2BT
Telephone: 01425 473305
Web: www.ringwoodraceway.com
Activities: archery, clay pigeon shooting, karting,
quad biking

Gorcombe Entertainments
Gorcombe Farm, Thornicombe
Nr Blandford DT11 9AG
Telephone: 01258 452219
Web: www.gorcombe.co.uk
Activities: clay pigeon shooting, paintballing, quad
biking

Wessex Sporting Events
624 Hillbutts, Wimborne BH21 4DS
Telephone: 0800 093 3530
Web: www.wessexsportingevents.com
Activities: archery, clay pigeon, Honda pilots, hovercrafts, paintballing, quad biking

Southern Counties Shooting
Wardon Hill, Nr Dorchester DT2 9PW
Telephone: 01935 83625
Web: www.southern-counties.com
Activities: clay pigeon shooting

Paintball
Master Blaster Paintball
39/4 Merryfield Park, Derritt Lane
Bransgore BH23 7AU
Telephone: 01202 201761
Web: www.bournemouth-paintball.co.uk

Challenge Paintball & Quad Bikes
248 Ringwood Road, St Leonards
Ringwood BH24 2SB
Telephone: 01202 877899

Scuba Diving
Divers Down (Swanage Ltd)
The Pier, Swanage BH19 2AN
Telephone: 01929 423565
Web: www.diversdown.tv

Skiing & Snowboarding
Christchurch Ski Centre
Matchams Lane, Hurn, Christchurch BH23 6AW
Telephone: 01202 499155
Web: www.christchurch-skicentre.com

Table-side Dancing Clubs
For Your Eyes Only
Old Christchurch Road, Bournemouth BH1 1NL
Telephone: 01202 311108
Website: www.fyeo.co.uk

Spearmint Rhino
1 Yelverton Road, Bournemouth BH1 1DA
Telephone: 01202 295300
Web: www.spearmintrhino.com

Tenpin Bowling
Superbowl
Glen Fern Road, Bournemouth BH1 2LZ
Telephone: 01202 291717
Web: www.megabowl.co.uk

The Dogs
Poole Stadium
Wimborne Road, Poole BH15 2BP
Telephone: 01202 677449
Web: www.poolegreyhounds.com

Watersports
Harbour Boardsailing
284 Sandbanks Road, Lilliput, Poole BH14 8HU
Telephone: 01202 700503
Web: www.pooleharbour.co.uk
Activities: windsurfing, kitesurfing

Hengistbury Head Centre
Broadway, Southbourne BH6 4EN
Telephone: 01202 425173
Activities: canoeing, kayaking, low ropes, sailing

Rockley Watersports
Rockley Point, Poole BH15 4RW
Telephone: 01202 677272
Web: www.rockleywatersports.com
Activities: sailing, powerboating, windsurfing

French Connection Watersports
4 Banks Road, Sandbanks, Poole BH13 7QB
Telephone: 01202 707757
Web: www.fcwatersports.co.uk
Activities: kitesurfing, windsurfing, wake boarding

Sail UK
29 Lulworth Avenue, Hanworthy, Poole BH15 4DQ
Telephone: 01202 668410
Web: www.sailuk.net

BRIGHTON

Tourist Information Centre
10 Bartholomew Square, Brighton BN1 1JS
Telephone: 0906 711 2255 (premium rate line,
calls cost 50p per minute)
Email: brighton-tourism@brighton-hove.gov.uk
Web: www.visitbrighton.com

Casinos
Grosvenor Casino
9 Grand Junction Road, Brighton BN1 1PP
Telephone: 01273 326514
Web: www.rank.com

Comedy Clubs
Check out www.whatson.brighton.co.uk for
listings.

Flying
Sussex Hang Gliding & Paragliding
Tollgate, Nr Lewes BN8 6JZ
Telephone: 01273 858170
Web: www.sussexhgpg.co.uk

Elite Helicopters
Hanger 3, Goodwood Airfield
Chichester PO18 0PH
Telephone: 01243 530165
Web: www.elitehelicopters.co.uk

Airbase Flying Club
The Old Customs Hall, Terminal Building
Shoreham Airport, Shoreham-by-Sea BN43 5FF
Telephone: 01273 455532
Web: www.airbaseflyingclub.co.uk

Golf
Brighton and Hove Golf Club
Devils Dyke Road, Brighton BN1 8YT
Telephone: 01273 556482

Horse Racing
Brighton Racecourse
Freshfield Road, Brighton BN2 9XZ
Telephone: 01273 603580
Web: www.brighton-racecourse.co.uk

Fontwell Racecourse
Fontwell, Arundel BN18 0SX
Telephone: 01243 543335
Web: www.fontwellpark.co.uk

Horse Riding
Beauport Park Riding School
Hastings Road, St Leonards-on-Sea TN38 8EA
Telephone: 01424 851424

Rottingdean Riding School
Chailey Avenue, Rottingdean BN2 7GH
Telephone: 01273 302155

Hot Air Ballooning
British School of Ballooning
Little London, Ebernoe, Nr Petworth GU28 9LF
Telephone: 01428 707307
Web: www.hotair.co.uk

Balloons Over Sussex
Greenacre Lodge, Breadstone, Berkeley GL13 9HF
Telephone: 01453 810018
Web: www.balloonsoversussex.co.uk

Karting
Trax Indoor Karting
46 Brampton Road, Hampden Park Industrial Estate
Eastbourne BN22 9AJ
Telephone: 01323 521133
Web: www.traxkarting.co.uk

Nightclubs
Babylon Lounge
Western Esplanade, Kingsway, Hove BN3 4FA
Telephone: 01273 207100

Creation
78 West Street, Brighton BN1 2RA
Telephone: 01273 321628
Web: www.applebelly.com

Outdoor Activity Centres
Madtrax Mudmania
Home Farm, Staplefield
Nr Haywards Heath RH17 6AP
Telephone: 01444 456441
Web: www.mudmania.co.uk
Activities: mudbuggies

Adventure Connections
Shelldale House, 3–9 Shelldale Road
Portslade BN41 1LE
Telephone: 01273 417007
Web: www.adventureconnections.co.uk
Activities: 4 x 4 driving, ballooning, banana boats,
canoeing, clay pigeon shooting, dinghy sailing,
flight simulator, flying, gliding, golf, hovercraft, jet
skiing, karting, murder mystery, off-road karting,
paintballing, paragliding, pleasure flights,
powerboating, power karts, power turns, quad
biking, scuba diving, tank driving, water skiing,
windsurfing, yacht sailing

Blackwool Farm
Colhook Common, Petworth GU28 9ND
Telephone: 01428 707258
Web: www.blackwoolfarm.co.uk
Activities: archery, clay pigeon shooting, fly-
fishing, hot air ballooning, karting, quad biking,
reverse steer driving

Q Leisure
London Road, Albourne, Hassocks BN6 9BQ
Telephone: 01273 834403
Web: www.qleisure.co.uk
Activities: 4 x 4 driving, archery, clay pigeon
shooting, karting, quad biking

Paintball
Demolition Paintball
28 Sompting Avenue (office)
Broadwater, Worthing BN14 8HN
Telephone: 01273 418263
Web: www.demolitionpaintball.co.uk

Shootout Paintball
Old Barn Farm, Cinderford Lane, Hellingly
Hailsham BN27 4HL
Telephone: 01424 777779
Web: www.shootout.uk.com

Scuba Diving
Sunstar Diving
160 South Street, Lancing BN15 8AU
Telephone: 01903 767224
Web: www.sunstardiving.co.uk

Skiing & Snowboarding
Knockhatch Ski Centre
Hempstead Lane, Hailsham BN27 3PR
Telephone: 01323 843344
Web: www.knockhatch.com

Table-side Dancing Clubs
Pussycats
The Basement, 176 Church Road, Hove BN3 2DJ
Telephone: 01273 709100
Web: www.pussycatclub.co.uk

Tenpin Bowling
Bowlplex
Brighton Marina, BN2 5UF
Telephone: 01273 818180
Web: www.bowlplexuk.com

The Dogs
Coral Brighton and Hove Greyhound Stadium
Neville Road, Hove BN3 7BZ
Telephone: 01273 204601
Web: www.coral.co.uk

Watersports
Hove Lagoon Watersports
Hove Lagoon, Kingsway, Hove BN3 4LX
Telephone: 01273 424842
Web: www.hovelagoon.co.uk

The Brighton Kayak Company
185 Kings Road Arches, Brighton BN1 1NB
Telephone: 01273 323160
Web: www.thebrightonkayak.co.uk

Winetasting
Brighton Wine School
9 Foundary Street, Brighton BN1 4AT
Telephone: 01273 672 525
Web: www.brightonwineschool.co.uk

BRISTOL

Tourist Information Centre
The Annexe, Wildscreen Walk
Harbourside, Bristol BS1 5DB
Telephone: 0117 926 0767 (Enquiries)
Email: ticharbourside@bristol-city.gov.uk
Web: www.visitbristol.co.uk

Casinos
Gala Casinos
Redcliffe Way, Bristol BS1 6NJ
Telephone: 0117 921 3189
Web: www.galacasinos.co.uk

Grosvenor Casino
266 Anchor Road, Bristol BS1 5TT
Telephone: 0117 929 2932
Web: www.rank.com

Comedy Clubs
Jesters Comedy Club
140–142 Cheltenham Road, Bristol BS6 5RL
Telephone: 0117 909 6655
Web: www.jesterscomedyclub.co.uk

Flying
Bristol Flying Centre
Bristol Airport, Lulsgate BS48 3DP
Telephone: 01275 474501
Web: www.b-f-c.co.uk

Bath, Wilts & North Dorset Gliding Club
The Park, Kingston Deverill, Warminster BA12 7HS
Telephone: 01985 844095
Web: www.bwnd.co.uk

Golf
Stockwood Vale Golf Club
Stockwood Lane, Bristol BS31 2ER
Telephone: 0117 986 6505
Web: www.stockwoodvale.com

Horse Racing
Cheltenham Racecourse
Prestbury Pk, Prestbury, Cheltenham GL50 4SH
Telephone: 01242 537642
Web: www.cheltenham.co.uk

Chepstow Racecourse
Chepstow, Monmouthsire NP16 6BE
Telephone: 01291 622260
Web: www.chepstow-racecourse.co.uk

Horse Riding
See High Action under Outdoor Activity Centres.

Gordano Valley Riding Centre
Moor Lane, Clapton In Gordano, Bristol BS20 7RF
Telephone: 01275 843473

Hot Air Ballooning
Balloons Over Bristol
Greenacre Lodge, Breadstone, Berkeley GL13 9HF
Telephone: 0117 985 9670
Web: www.balloonsoverbristol.co.uk

First Flight
Telephone: 0117 973 1073
Web: www.firstflight.co.uk

Karting
The Raceway
Avonmouth Way, Avonmouth BS11 9YA
Telephone: 0800 376 6111
Web: www.theraceway.co.uk

West Country Karting
Trench Lane, Winterbourne BS36 1RY
Telephone: 01454 202666
Web: www.westcountrykarting.co.uk

Nightclubs
Brannigans
Harbourside, Canons Way, Bristol BS1 5UH
Telephone: 0117 927 7863

Evolution
Waterfront, Canons Road, Bristol BS1 5UH
Telephone: 0117 922 0330

The Works
15 Nelson Street, Bristol BS1 2JY
Telephone: 0117 929 2658
Web: www.applebelly.com

Outdoor Activity Centres
High Action
Lyncombe Drive, Churchill, Nr Somerset BS25 5PQ
Telephone: 01934 852335
Web: www.highaction.co.uk
Activities: 4 x 4 off-road driving, abseiling, archery,

climbing, dry slope skiing, horse riding, mountain
biking, quad biking, snowboarding

Chepstow Outdoor Activity Centre
Tump Farm, Sedbury, Chepstow NP16 7HN
Telephone: 01291 629901
Web: www.chepstowoutdooractivities.co.uk
Activities: 4 x 4 driving, archery, clay pigeon
shooting, paintballing, quad biking, sphere-mania
(zorbing)

BHP Inspiring Events
The Old Stables, Box Hedge Farm
Coalpit Heath BS36 2UW
Telephone: 01454 775541
Web: www.stag-hen-party.com
Activities: archery, clay pigeon shooting, Honda
pilots, karting, max kats, quad biking, tank driving

T Z Paintball
Weston Lodge Farm, Valley Road, Portishead
Telephone: 01934 416507
Web: www.tzpaintball.co.uk
Activities: clay pigeon shooting, off-road karting,
paintballing, quad biking

Bristol Outdoor Pursuits Centre
Common Wood, Huntstrete, Pensford BS39 4NT
Telephone: 0800 980 3980
Web: www.bristoloutdoor.co.uk
Activities: Honda pilots, paintballing, quad biking

Paintball
Paintball Adventures (Brockley Combe)
31 Hopps Road, Kingswood BS15 9QQ
Telephone: 0117 935 3300
Web: www.paintball-adventures.co.uk

Skiing & Snowboarding
See High Action under Outdoor Activity Centres.

Table-side Dancing Clubs
Club Crème
46 West Street, St Philips (Old Market)
Bristol BS2 0BH
Telephone: 0117 914 0049
Web: www.clubcreme.com

Tenpin Bowling
Megabowl
Brunel Way, Ashton Gate, Bristol BS3 2YX
Telephone: 0117 953 8538
Web: www.megabowl.co.uk

Watersports
See Cotswold Water Park under Watersports for Bath

CARDIFF

Cardiff Visitor Centre
16 Wood Street, Cardiff CF10 1ES
Telephone: 02920 227281
Email: visitor@thecardiffinitiative.co.uk
Web: www.cardiffvisitor.info

Casinos
Grosvenor Casino
Greyfriars Road, Cardiff CF10 3AD
Telephone: 02920 342991
Web: www.rank.com

Comedy Clubs
Jongleurs
Units 1 & 5, Ground & 1st Floor
Millennium Plaza, Wood Street, Cardiff CF10 1LA
Telephone: 0870 240 2731
Web: www.jongleurs.co.uk

Golf
Cottrell Park Golf Club
St Nicholas, Cardiff CF5 6SJ
Telephone: 01446 781781
Web: www.cottrell-park.co.uk

Peterstone Lakes Golf Club
Peterstone, Wentlooge, Cardiff CF3 2TN
Telephone: 01633 680075
Web: www.peterstonelakes.com

Horse Racing
Chepstow Racecourse
Chepstow NP16 6BE
Telephone: 01291 622260
Web: www.chepstow-racecourse.co.uk

Hot Air Ballooning
Balloons Over Wales
Greenacre Lodge, Breadstone, Berkeley GL13 9HF
Telephone: 01453 810018
Web: www.balloonsoverwales.co.uk

Karting
South Wales Karting Centre
Llandow Circuit, Llandow Trading Estate
Cowbridge CF71 7PB
Telephone: 01446 795568
Web: www.stathankartclub.com

Nightclubs
Evolution
Atlantic Wharf, Hemmingway Road
Cardiff CF10 4JY
Telephone: 02920 464444

Flares
96 St Mary Street, Cardiff CF10 1DX
Telephone: 02920 235825

Surfers Nightclub
Millennium Plaza, Wood Street, Cardiff CF10 1LA
Telephone: 02920 377178
Web: www.regentinns.co.uk

Outdoor Activity Centres
Taff Valley Buggy Trail & Activity Centre
Cwrt-y-celyn Farm, Upper Boat
Pontypridd CF37 5BJ
Telephone: 02920 831658
Web: www.adventurewales.co.uk
Activities: 4 x 4 driving, archery, assault courses,
clay pigeon shooting, orienteering, pony trekking,
quad biking

Merlin Adventures
71 Ty Cerrig, Pentwyn, Cardiff CF2 7DQ
Telephone: 02920 549640
Activities: abseiling, caving, gorge scrambling, hill
walking & mountaineering, improvised rafting,
kayaking, open canoeing, rock climbing

Also see Taskforce Paintball Games under
Paintball

Paintball
Taskforce Paintball Games
Llanedos Street, Lythans, Cardiff CF5 6BQ
Telephone: 02920 593900
Web: www.taskforcepaintball.co.uk
Activities: archery, falconry, laser clay shooting,
paintballing

Skiing & Snowboarding
Cardiff Ski Centre
Fairwater Road, Cardiff CF5 3JR
Telephone: 02920 561793
Web: www.skicardiff.com

Table-side Dancing
The Fantasy Lounge
93 St Mary Street, Cardiff CF10
Telephone: 02920 382201

Tenpin Bowling
Megabowl
Newport Road, Cardiff CF23 9AE
Telephone: 02920 461666
Web: www.megabowl.co.uk

Watersports
Ocean Quest Watersports Centre
Unit 7 West Bute Street, Cardiff CF1 6EP
Telephone: 02920 303545
Web: www.ocean-quest.co.uk

Llanishen Sailing Centre
Llanishen Reservoir, Lisvane Road, Llanishen CF4 5SE
Telephone: 02920 761360
Web: www.llanishensc.connectfree.co.uk

EDINBURGH

Tourist Information Office
3 Princes Street, Edinburgh EH2 2QP
Telephone: 0845 225 5121
Email: info@visitscotland.com
Web: www.edinburgh.org

Casinos
Gala Casino
5 South Maybury Road, Edinburgh EH12 8NE
Telephone: 0131 338 4444
Web: www.galacasinos.co.uk

Comedy Clubs
The Stand Comedy Club
5 York Place, Edinburgh EH1 3EB
Telephone: 0131 558 7272
Web: www.thestand.co.uk

Flying
Scotia Helicopters
Cumbernauld Airport, Cumbernauld G68 0HH
Telephone: 01236 780140
Web: www.scotiahelicopters.co.uk

Microlight Scotland
Cumbernauld Airport, Cumbernauld G68 0HH
Telephone: 07979 971301
Web: www.microlightscotland.com

Golf
Kings Acre Golf Course & Academy
Lasswade, Midlothian EH18 1AU
Telephone: 0131 663 3456
Web: www.kings-acregolf.com

Horse Racing
Musselburgh Racecourse
Linkfield Road, Musselburgh EH21 7RG
Telephone: 0131 665 2859
Web: www.musselburgh-racecourse.co.uk

Horse Riding
Pentland Hills Icelandics
Windy Gowl Farm, Carlops, Penicuik EH26 9NL
Telephone: 01968 661095
Web: www.phicelandics.co.uk

Hot Air Ballooning
Balloons Over Scotland
Greenacre Lodge, Breadstone, Berkeley GL13 9HF
Telephone: 01453 810018
Web: www.balloonsoverscotland.co.uk

Karting
Racing Karts
Arrol Square, Livingston EH54 8QZ
Telephone: 01506 410123
Web: www.racingkarts.co.uk

Fastrax Motorsports
Inzievar Oakley
Telephone: 01383 880300
Web: www.fastrax.org

Nightclubs
Revolution
31 Lothian Road, Edinburgh EH1 2DJ
Telephone: 0131 229 7670
Web: www.revolution-edinburgh.co.uk

Subway Nightclub
69 Cowgate, Edinburgh EH1 1JW
Telephone: 0131 225 6766
Web: www.subwayclubs.co.uk

The Basement (late night bar)
10A Broughton Street, Edinburgh EH1 3RH
Telephone: 0131 557 0097
Web: www.thebasement.org.uk

Outdoor Activity Centres
Mavis Hall Park
Humbie, East Lothian EH36 5PL
Telephone: 01875 833733
Web: www.mavishallpark.co.uk
Activities: archery, blindfold driving, clay pigeon
shooting, falconry, Highland games, off-road
driving, quad biking, reverse steer driving

Cluny Clays Activity Centre
Cluny, Kirkcaldy KY2 6QU
Telephone: 01592 720374
Web: www.clunyclays.co.uk
Activities: 9 hole golf course, 27 bay driving range,
archery & air rifle facilities, clay pigeon shooting,
falconry, Honda Pilots, quad biking, reverse steer
Land Rover driving

Nae Limits
Tay Terrace, Dunkeld PH8 0AQ
Telephone: 01350 727242
Web: www.naelimits.com
Activities: canyonning, cliff jumping, duckie trips,
gorge crossing, skiing, rap running (forwards
abseiling), river bugs, white-water rafting

Bedlam Event Management
28 Great King Street, Edinburgh EH3 6QH
Telephone: 07000 233526
Web: www.bedlam.co.uk
Activities: 4 x 4 off-road driving, archery, clay
pigeon shooting, Honda pilots, karting,
paintballing, quad biking, rally driving

Paintball
Skirmish Scotland
Gateside Commerce Park
Haddington, East Lothian EH14 3ST
Telephone: 0131 477 9661
Web: www.skirmishscotland.co.uk

Skiing & Snowboarding
Midlothian Ski Centre
Hillend, Edinburgh EH10 7DU
Telephone: 0131 445 4433
Web: www.ski.midlothian.gov.uk

Table-side Dancing Clubs
Bottoms Up
93 Lothian Road, Edinburgh EH3 9AW
Telephone: 0131 229 1599
Web: www.bottomsupshowbar.co.uk

Hooters
2 Lauriston Street, Edinburgh EH3 9DJ
Telephone: 0131 228 9996
Web: www.hootersclub.com

Tenpin Bowling
Megabowl
Fountain Bridge, Dundee Street
Edinburgh EH11 1AW
Telephone: 0870 850 8000
Web: www.megabowl.co.uk

Watersports
Port Edgar Sailing School and Marina
Shore Road, South Queensferry EH30 9SQ
Telephone: 0131 331 3330
Web: www.portedgar.com

Loch Insh Watersports & Skiing Centre
(2hrs from Edinburgh)
Insh Hall, Kincraig PH21 1NU
Telephone: 01540 651272
Web: www.lochinsh.com

GLASGOW

Greater Glasgow & Clyde Valley Tourist Board
11 George Square, Glasgow G2 1DY
Telephone: 0141 204 4480
Web: www.seeglasgow.com

Casinos
Gala Casinos
Various venues around Glasgow.
Web: www.galacasinos.co.uk

Comedy Clubs
Jongleurs
UGC Dev., 11 Renfrew Street, Glasgow G2 3AB
Telephone: 0870 240 3417
Web: www.jongleurs.co.uk

Flying
Glasgow Flying Club
Glasgow International Airport
Walkinshaw Road, Renfrew PA4 9LP
Telephone: 0141 889 4565
Web: www.glasgowflyingclub.com

Scotia Helicopters
Cumbernauld Airport, Cumbernauld G68 0HH
Telephone: 01236 780140
Web: www.scotiahelicopters.co.uk

Microlight Scotland
Cumbernauld Airport, Cumbernauld G68 0HH
Telephone: 07979 971301
Web: www.microlightscotland.com

Golf
Alexandra Golf Course
Alexandra Parade, Glasgow G31 3BS
Telephone: 0141 556 1294

Knightswood Golf Course
Lincoln Avenue, Glasgow G13 3RH
Telephone: 0141 959 6358

Horse Racing
Hamilton Park Racecourse
Bothwell Road, Hamilton ML3 0DW
Telephone: 01698 283806
Website: www.hamilton-park.co.uk

Horse Riding
Ardgowan Riding Centre
Bankfoot, Inverkip, Greenock PA16 0DT
Telephone: 01475 521390
Web: www.ardgowan-riding.co.uk

Hot Air Ballooning
Balloons Over Scotland
Greenacre Lodge, Breadstone, Berkeley GL13 9HF
Telephone: 01453 810018
Web: www.balloonsoverscotland.co.uk

Karting
Scotkart Indoor Racing
Westburn Road, Cambuslang G72 7UD
Telephone: 0141 641 0222
Web: www.scotkart.co.uk

Nightclubs
Lowdown
158–164 Bath Street, Glasgow G2 4TB
Telephone: 0141 331 4060

The Shed
26 Langside Avenue, Shawlands, Glasgow G41 2QS
Telephone: 0141 649 5020
Web: www.shedglasgow.co.uk

Victorias
98 Sauchiehall Street, Glasgow G2 3DE
Telephone: 0141 332 1444
Web: www.victoriasglasgow.com

Outdoor Activity Centres
Active Outdoor Pursuits
Stayamrie, Benston Road, Cumnock
Ayrshire KA18 4PJ
Telephone: 01540 673319
Web: www.activeoutdoorpursuits.com
Activities: abseiling, canoeing, canyoning and
gorge walking, hill walking, mountain biking,
mountaineering, rock climbing, rope courses,
skiing & snowboarding, ski mountaineering,
white-water rafting

Also see Nae Limits and Bedlam Event
Management under the Outdoor Activity Centres
for Edinburgh

Paintball
Scottish Paintball Centre
Meiklemosside, Fenwick KA3 6AY
Telephone: 0141 423 9199
Web: www.scottishpaintballcentre.co.uk

Scuba Diving
Aquatron Dive Centre
30 Stanley Street, Kinning Park G41 1JB
Telephone: 0141 429 7575
Web: www.aquatron.co.uk

Skiing & Snowboarding
Glasgow Bearsden Ski Club
The Mound, Stockiemuir Road, Bearsden G61 3RS
Telephone: 0141 943 1500
Web: www.skibearsden.co.uk

Table-side Dancing Clubs
Legs 'n' Co
86 Maxwell Street, Glasgow G1 4EQ
Telephone: 0141 221 4657
Web: www.legsnco.com

Tenpin Bowling
AMF Bowling
Elliott Street, Glasgow G3 8DZ
Telephone: 0141 248 4478
Web: www.amfbowling.co.uk

The Dogs
Shawfield Greyhound Stadium
Rutherglen Road, Glasgow G73 1SZ
Telephone: 0141 647 4121
Web: www.thedogs.co.uk

Watersports
Galloway Sailing & Watersports Centre
Parton, Loch Ken, Kirkcudbrightshire
Dumfries DG7 3NQ
Telephone: 01644 420626
Web: www.lochken.co.uk

LEEDS

Gateway Yorkshire Leeds Regional Travel & Tourist
Information Centre
Telephone: 0113 242 5242
Email: tourinfo@leeds.gov.uk
Web: www.leeds.gov.uk

Casinos
Gala Casinos
Wellington Bridge Street, Westgate, Leeds LS3 1LW
Telephone: 0113 389 3700
Web: www.galacasinos.co.uk

Grosvenor Casino
Podium Building, Merrion Way, Leeds LS2 8BT
Telephone: 0113 244 8386
Web: www.rank.com

Grosvenor Casino
Moortown Corner House, 343 Harrogate Road
Leeds LS17 6LD
Telephone: 0113 269 5051
Web: www.rank.com

Comedy Clubs
Jongleurs
The Cube, Units 1, 2 & 4, Albion Street
Leeds LS2 8PN
Telephone: 0113 247 1759
Web: www.jongleurs.co.uk

Flying
Airborne Hang Gliding & Paragliding Centre
The Ranch, Hey End Farm, Luddendenfoot
Halifax HX2 6JN
Telephone: 01422 834989
Web: www.airborne.uk.com

Leeds Flying School
Unit 84, Coney Park Estate
Leeds Bradford International Airport
Harrogate Road, Leeds LS19 7XS
Telephone: 0845 166 2506
Web: www.leedsflyingschool.co.uk

Golf
Oulton Park Golf Club
Rothwell Lane, Leeds LS26 8EX
Telephone: 0113 282 3152
Web: www.leeds.gov.uk

Temple Newsam Golf Club
Temple Newsam, Leeds LS15 0NL
Telephone: 0113 264 7362
Web: www.leeds.gov.uk

Roundhay Golf Club
Park Lane, Leeds LS8 2EJ
Telephone: 0113 266 1686
Web: www.leeds.gov.uk

Horse Racing
Wetherby Racecourse
York Road, Wetherby LS22 5EJ
Telephone: 01937 582035
Web: www.wetherbyracing.co.uk

Horse Riding
Yorkshire Riding Centre
Markington, Harrogate HG3 3PD
Telephone: 01765 677207
Web: www.yrc.co.uk

Hot Air Ballooning
Balloons Over Yorkshire
Greenacre Lodge, Breadstone, Berkeley GL13 9HF
Telephone: 01453 810018
Web: www.balloonsoveryorkshire.co.uk

Karting
Pole Position Indoor Karting
Sayner Lane, Leeds LS10 1LS
Telephone: 0113 243 3775
Web: www.polepositionindoorkarting.co.uk

Kart Skill
Riverside Raceway, South Accommodation Road
Hunslet LS9 9AS
Telephone: 0113 249 1000
Web: www.kartskill.co.uk

Nightclubs
Bird Cage Nightclub
52–56 Boar Lane, Leeds LS1 5EL
Telephone: 0113 246 7273
Web: www.birdcagelive.com

Baja Beach Club
43A Woodhouse Lane, Leeds LS2 8JT
Telephone: 0113 245 4088
Web: www.bajabeachclub.co.uk

Majestyk & Jumpin Jaks
City Square, Leeds LS1 4DS
Telephone: 0113 242 4333
Web: www.ukcn.com

Bondi Beach
Queens Buildings, City Square, Leeds LS1 4DS
Telephone: 0113 243 4744

Mint Club
8 Harrison Street, Leeds LS1 6PA
Telephone: 0113 244 3168
Web: www.themintclubleeds.co.uk

Heaven and Hell
9 Grand Arcade, Merrion Street, Leeds LS1 6PQ
Telephone: 0113 243 9963
Web: www.heavenandhell.co.uk

Evolution
Cardigan Fields Leisure Park
Kirkstall Road, Leeds LS4 2DG
Telephone: 0113 263 2632

Outdoor Activity Centres
Stagandhenweekend.com
Holme View, Ilkley LS29 9EL
Telephone: 01943 609334
Web: www.stagandhenweekend.com
Activities: abseiling, clay pigeon shooting,
climbing, karting, off-road driving, paintballing,
quad biking, rafting

Banana Chilli
233 Keighley Road, Cowling, Keighley BD22 0AA
Telephone: 01535 637000
Web: www.bananachilli.co.uk
Activities: 4 x 4 driving, abseiling, archery,
bungee jumping, canoeing, caving, clay pigeon
shooting, climbing, gladiators, golf, gorge
walking, Honda pilots, horse riding, hot air
ballooning, hovercrafts, karting, mountain biking,

paintballing, quad biking, rodeo bull, scuba experience, skiing, snowboarding, sumo, waterskiing, white-water rafting

North of England Activity Centre
Tinker Lane, Harewood Whin, Rufforth
York YO23 3RR
Telephone: 01904 738120
Web: www.noeac.co.uk
Activities: 4 x 4 off-road driving, archery, clay pigeon shooting, grass kart racing, quad biking

Paintball
Paintball Commando
Castle Farm, Milnthorpe Lane, Sandal
Wakefield WF2 7JA
Telephone: 01924 252123
Web: www.paintballcommando.co.uk

Scuba Diving
Bear Divers
3 Stannigley Road, Armley, Leeds LS12 3AP
Telephone: 0113 217 2800
Web: www.beardivers.co.uk

Skiing & Snowboarding
See Sheffield Ski Village under Skiing and Snowboarding for Sheffield

Table-side Dancing Clubs
Purple Door
5 York Place, Leeds LS1 2DR
Telephone: 0113 245 0556
Web: www.purpledoorleeds.com

Spearmint Rhino
1 Oxford Street, Harrogate HG1 1PY
Telephone: 01423 540540
Web: www.spearmintrhino.com

Tenpin Bowling
AMF Bowling Leeds
Merrion Centre, Leeds LS2 8BT
Telephone: 0113 245 1781
Web: www.amfbowling.co.uk

The Dogs
Kinsley Greyhound Stadium
96 Wakefield Road, Kinsley, Pontefract WF9 5EH
Telephone: 01977 610946
Web: www.kinsleydogs.co.uk

Watersports
Leeds Sailing, Canoeing & Kayaking Centre
Yeadon Tarn, Leeds LS19
Telephone: 0113 250 3616
Web: www.leeds.gov.uk

LIVERPOOL

Tourist Information Centre
Atlantic Pavilion, Albert Dock, Liverpool L1 1RG
Telephone: 0906 680 6886 (calls cost 25p per min)
Email: askme@visitliverpool.com
Web: www.visitliverpool.com

Casinos
Grosvenor Casino
76–78 West Derby Road, Liverpool L6 9BY
Telephone: 0151 260 8199
Web: www.rank.com

Comedy Clubs
Rawhide Comedy Club @ Baby Blue
PO Box 23, Liverpool L17 8FR
Telephone: 0151 726 0077
Web: www.rawhidecomedy.com

Flying
See Lancashire Aero Club under Flying for Manchester

Golf

Bootle Golf Course
Dunnings Bridge Road, Liverpool L30 2PP
Telephone: 0151 928 1371

Childwall Golf Club
Naylors Road, Liverpool L27 2YB
Telephone: 0151 487 9871

Horse Racing

Aintree Racecourse
Ormskirk Road, Liverpool L9 5AS
Telephone: 0151 522 2929
Web: www.aintree.co.uk

Haydock Park Racecourse
Newton-Le-Willows WA12 0HQ
Telephone: 01942 402624
Web: www.haydock-park.com

Horse Riding

Foxes Riding School
Badgers Rake Lane, Ledsham, Wirral CH66 8PF
Telephone: 0151 339 6797
Web: www.ridingschools.co.uk

Hot Air Ballooning

Balloons Over The Mersey
Greenacre Lodge, Breadstone, Berkeley GL13 9HF
Telephone: 01453 810018
Web: www.balloonsoverthemersey.co.uk

Karting

Mersey Karting
Unit 1, Paragon Centre, Piction Road, Wavertree
Liverpool L15 4LP
Telephone: 0151 734 1736
Web: www.merseykarting.co.uk

Nightclubs

Garlands
Telephone: 0151 709 9586
Web: www.garlandsonline.co.uk

Club 051
1 Mount Pleasant, Liverpool L3 5SX
Telephone: 0151 707 8385
Web: www.theclub051.co.uk

Bar-celona
35 Renshaw Street, Liverpool
Telephone: 0151 709 0880
Web: www.bar-celona.co.uk

The Krazyhouse
16 Wood Street, Liverpool L1 4AQ
Telephone: 0151 708 5016
Web: www.thekrazyhouse.co.uk

Outdoor Activity Centres

Adventure 21
21 Babylon Lane, Anderton, Chorley PR6 9NR
Telephone: 01257 474467
Web: www.adventure21.co.uk
Activities: aquaseiling, abseiling, canoeing, caving,
canyoning, climbing, culvert scrambling, gorge
scrambling, kayaking, mountain biking,
orienteering, raft building, windsurfing

Pro Adventure
23 Castle Street, Llangollen LL20 8NY
Telephone: 01978 861912
Web: www.adventureholiday.com
Activities: abseiling, canoeing, canyoning, gorge
walking, kayaking, mountain biking, rock
climbing, white-water rafting

Itcar Clay Pigeon Club
Altcar Range, Hightown, Near Formby
Telephone: 0151 924 5921
Activities: clay pigeon shooting

Paintball
SWAT Paintball Activities
84 Parkside Road, Bebington CH63 7NR
Telephone: 0151 644 1611
Web: www.swatpaintball.co.uk

Paintball Zone (Knowsley)
46 Garthdale Road
Liverpool
L18 5HW
Telephone: 0151 735 0011
Web: www.paintballzone.co.uk

Skiing & Snowboarding
Runcorn Ski and Snowboard Centre
Town Park, Palace Fields, Runcorn WA7 2PS
Telephone: 01928 701965
Web: www.runcornskicentre.co.uk

Table-side Dancing Clubs
Aphrodites
11–17 Harrington Street, Liverpool L2 9QA
Telephone: 0151 227 4154
Web: www.aphrodites-liverpool.co.uk

Tenpin Bowling
Megabowl
Switch Island Leisure Park, Dunnings Bridge Road
Bootle L30 6TQ
Telephone: 0151 525 5676
Web: www.megabowl.co.uk

The Dogs
See Belle Vue Greyhound Stadium under The Dogs
for Manchester

Watersports
Wirral Sailing & Watersports Centre
West Kirby Marine Lake, South Parade
West Kirby CH48 0GQ
Telephone: 0151 625 2510
Web: www.wirral.gov.uk

Surf-Tech
Crosby Marina, Liverpool L22 5PT
Telephone: 0151 920 8855
Web: www.surf-tech.co.uk
Activities: dinghy sailing, kitesurfing, waterskiing,
windsurfing

LONDON

London Visitor Centre
Arrivals Hall, Waterloo International Terminal
London SE1 7LT
Telephone: 0905 123 5000 (calls charged at £1
per minute)
Web: www.londontouristboard.com

Casinos
Gala Casinos
1 Baker Street, London W1M 1AA
Telephone: 020 7935 5013
Web: www.galacasinos.co.uk

The Grosvenor Victoria
150–162 Edgware Road, London W2 2DT
Telephone: 020 7262 7777
Web: www.rank.com

Comedy Clubs
The Comedy Store
1A Oxendon Street, London SW1Y 4EE
Telephone: 020 7344 0234
Web: www.thecomedystore.co.uk

Jongleurs
49 Lavender Gardens, Battersea, London SW11 1DJ
Telephone: 0870 240 2398
Web: www.jongleurs.co.uk

Jongleurs
Bow Wharf, 221 Grove Road, Bow, London E3 1AA
Telephone: 0870 240 2447
Web: www.jongleurs.co.uk

Jongleurs
11 East Yard, Camden Lock, London NW1 8AF
Telephone: 0870 240 2476
Web: www.jongleurs.co.uk

Flying
The Cabair Group Ltd (for a variety of locations)
Elstree Aerodrome, Boreham Wood WD6 3AW
Telephone: 020 8236 2400
Web: www.cabair.com

Golf
Trent Park Public Golf Club
Bramley Road, Southgate N14 4UW
Telephone: 020 8367 4653
Web: www.trentparkgolfclub.com

Lee Valley Leisure Golf Course
Picketts Lock Lane, Edmonton N9 0AS
Telephone: 020 8803 3611

Central London Golf Centre
Burntwood Lane, Wandsworth SW17 0AT
Telephone: 020 8871 2468
Web: www.clgc.co.uk

Horse Racing
Ascot Racecourse
Ascot, Berkshire SL5 7JX
Telephone: 01344 876876
Web: www.ascot.co.uk

Epsom Downs Racecourse
Epsom Downs, Epsom KT18 5LQ
Telephone: 01372 470047
Web: www.epsomderby.co.uk

Windsor Racecourse
The Racecourse, Maidenhead Road, Windsor SL4 5JJ
Telephone: 0870 200 0024
Web: www.windsor-racecourse.co.uk

Kempton Park Racecourse
Kempton Park, Staines Road East
Sunbury-On-Thames TW16 5AQ
Telephone: 01372 470047
Web: www.kempton.co.uk

Sandown Park Racecourse
Portsmouth Road, Esher KT10 9AJ
Telephone: 01372 470047
Web: www.sandown.co.uk

Horse Riding
Ridgway Stables
93 Ridgway, Wimbledon Village, London SW19 4SU
Telephone: 020 8946 7400
Web: www.ridgwaystables.co.uk

Ross Nye Stables
8 Bathurst Mews, London W2 2SB
Telephone: 020 7262 3791
Web: www.ridingstables.co.uk

Lee Valley Riding Centre
Lee Valley Regional Park, Lee Bridge Road
Leyton, London E10 7QL
Telephone: 020 8556 2629
Web: www.leevalleypark.com

Hot Air Ballooning
Balloons Over London
Greenacre Lodge, Breadstone, Berkeley GL13 9HF
Telephone: 01453 810018
Web: www.balloonsoverlondon.co.uk

British School of Ballooning
Little London, Ebernoe, Nr Petworth GU28 9LF
Telephone: 01428 707307
Web: www.hotair.co.uk

Karting
Streatham Kart Raceway
390 Streatham High Road, London SW16 6HX
Telephone: 020 8677 8677
Web: www.playscape.co.uk/karting

Daytona London
Union Gate, Atlas Road, Park Royal
London NW10 6DN
Telephone: 0845 644 5501
Web: www.daytona.co.uk

Nightclubs
Break for the Border
8–9 Argyll Street, London W1F 7TF
Telephone: 020 7734 5776
Web: www.bftb.com

The Clapham Grand
21–25 St. John's Hill, London SW11 1TT
Telephone: 020 7223 6523
Web: www.leopardclubs.com

Walkabout
136 Shaftesbury Avenue, London W1D 5EZ
Telephone: 020 7434 0572
Web: www.walkabout.eu.com

School Disco
Telephone: 08717 177475
Web: www.schooldisco.com

Outdoor Activity Centres
Combat Games
Henfold Lakes, Beare Green, Dorking RH5 4RW
Telephone: 0870 745 0756
Web: www.ukpaintballgames.com

Activities: archery, axe throwing(!?), crossbows, mud karting, paintballing, quad biking, raft building, sling shot

Lee Leisure
84A Luton Road, Charlton, Luton LU4 9UD
Telephone: 01525 876774
Web: www.lee-leisure.co.uk
Activities: archery, clay pigeon shooting, golf

West London Shooting School
Sharvel Lane, West End Road, Northolt UB5 6RA
Telephone: 020 8845 1377
Web: www.shootingschool.co.uk
Activities: 4 x 4 off-road driving, archery, clay pigeon shooting, quad biking, Honda pilots and reverse steer, sniper rifles
No alcohol and no fancy dress.

Quad Safari
P.O. Box 101, Ware SG11 1WA
Telephone: 01920 822977
Web: www.quadsafari.co.uk
Activities: 4 x 4 driving, quad biking

Paintball
City Paintball
Telephone: 0700 2 7529 2255
Web: www.citypaintball.com

Paintzone
393 Selsdon Road, South Croydon CR2 7AW
Telephone: 020 8688 1118
Web: www.paintzone.co.uk

Weekend Warriors (Cane End near Reading)
13–21 Crown Street, Reading RG1 2SE
Telephone: 0800 195 0637
Web: www.weekend-warriors.co.uk

National Paintball Parks
Stocking Wood, Pembridge Lane, Broxbourne EN10
and
Street End Copse, Hook Road, Rotherwick
Hook RG27
Telephone: 01707 660088
Web: www.paintballparks.co.uk

Pampering
The Refinery (men only)
60 Brook Street, Mayfair, London W1Y 1YB
Telephone: 020 7409 2001
Web: www.the-refinery.com

Polo
Ascot Park Polo Club
Windlesham Road, Chobham GU24 8SN
Telephone: 01276 858545
Web: www.polo.co.uk

Epsom Polo Club
Horton Country Park, Horton Lane, Epsom KT19 8PL
Telephone: 01372 749490
Web: www.epsompoloclub.co.uk

Scuba Diving
London School of Diving
11 Power Road, London W4 5PT
Telephone: 020 8995 0002
Web: www.londonschoolofdiving.co.uk

Skiing & Snowboarding
Wycombe Summit
Abbey Barn Lane, High Wycombe HP10 9QQ
Telephone: 01494 474711
Web: www.wycombesummit.com

Snow Zone
Xscape, 602 Marlborough Gate
Milton Keynes MK9 2XS
Telephone: 01908 230260
Web: www.xscape.co.uk

Table-side Dancing Clubs
Browns
1 Hackney Road, Shoreditch, London E2 7NX
Telephone: 020 7739 4653
Web: www.browns-griffin.co.uk

For Your Eyes Only
11 White Horse Street, Mayfair, London W1Y 7LB
Telephone: 020 7499 6816
Web: www.fyeo.co.uk

For Your Eyes Only
28 Abbey Road, Park Royal, London NW10 7SB
Telephone: 020 8965 7699
Web: www.fyeo.co.uk

Secrets (various venues around London)
Web: www.secrets-clubs.com

Spearmint Rhino
161 Tottenham Court Road, London W1T 7NN
Telephone: 020 7209 4488
Web: www.spearmintrhino.com

Tenpin Bowling
Megabowl
142 Streatham Hill, London SW2 4RU
Telephone: 020 8678 6007
Web: www.megabowl.co.uk

Megabowl
The Rotunda, Clarence Street
Kingston Upon Thames KT1 1QP
Telephone: 020 8547 4210
Web: www.megabowl.co.uk

The Dogs
Catford Stadium
Adenmore Road, Catford, London SE6 4RJ
Telephone: 020 8690 8000
Web: www.catfordstadium.co.uk

Walthamstow Stadium
Chingford Road, London E4 8SJ
Telephone: 020 8498 3300
Web: www.wsgreyhound.co.uk

Wimbledon Stadium
Plough Lane, London SW17 0BL
Telephone: 020 8946 8000
Web: www.wimbledondogs.co.uk

Watersports
The Docklands Sailing & Watersports Centre
235A Westferry Road, Millwall Dock
Isle of Dogs E14 3QS
Telephone: 020 7537 2626
Web: www.dswc.org

Surrey Docks Watersports Centre
Rope Street, London SE16 7SX
Telephone: 020 7237 5555

Bella Tours
74 Alder Lodge, River Gardens
73 Stevenage Road, London SW6 6NR
Telephone: 07010 711855
Web: www.bella-tours.com

Classic Charters
Mimosa, Mill Stream Moorings
Mill Lane, Windsor SL4 5JH
Telephone: 01753 861494
Web: www.classic-yacht-charters.com

Winetasting
Vinopolis
1 Bank End, London SE1 9BU
Telephone: 0870 241 4040
Web: www.vinopolis.co.uk

MANCHESTER

Visitor Centre
Town Hall Extension, Lloyd Street
Manchester M60 2LA
Telephone: 0161 234 3157
Web: www.destinationmanchester.com

Casinos
Grosvenor Casino
2 Empire Street, Cheetham Hill
Manchester M3 1JA
Telephone: 0161 834 8433
Web: www.rank.com

Grosvenor Casino
35–39 George Street, Manchester M1 4HQ
Telephone: 0161 236 7121
Web: www.rank.com

Comedy Clubs
The Comedy Store
Deansgate Lock, Manchester M1
Telephone: 0870 593 2932
Web: www.thecomedystore.co.uk

Jongleurs
40 Chorlton Street, Manchester M1 3HW
Telephone: 0870 240 2481
Web: www.jongleurs.co.uk

Flying
Lancashire Aero Club
Barton Aerodrome, Liverpool Road, Eccles M30 7SA
Telephone: 0161 787 7326
Web: www.lancsaeroclub.co.uk

MSF Aviation
Business Aviation Centre, Hanger 7
Manchester Airport West, Manchester M90 5NE
Telephone: 0161 436 0123
Web: www.msf-aviation.com

Golf
Heaton Park Golf Centre
Middleton Road, Prestwich M25 2SW
Telephone: 0161 654 9899

Horse Racing
Haydock Park Racecourse
Newton-Le-Willows WA12 0HQ
Telephone: 01942 402624
Web: www.haydock-park.com

Chester Racecourse
Watergate Square, Chester CH1 2LY
Telephone: 01244 304600
Web: www.chester-races.co.uk

Horse Riding
Ashton Hall Equestrian Centre
Church Lane, Ashton-on-Mersey
Telephone: 0161 905 3160

Hot Air Ballooning
Balloons Over Manchester
Greenacre Lodge, Breadstone, Berkeley GL13 9HF
Telephone: 01453 810018
Web: www.balloonsovermanchester.co.uk

Karting
Karting 2000
27 Froxmer Street, Gorton M18 8EF
Telephone: 0161 231 2000
Web: www.karting2000.co.uk
Also provide clay pigeon shooting and paint ball.

C K Karting
The Mill, Water Street, Radcliffe M26 3WE
Telephone: 0161 723 1010
Web: www.cat1karting.co.uk

Nightclubs
The Ritz Nightclub
Whitworth Street West, Manchester M1 5NQ
Telephone: 0161 236 4355
Web: www.theritznightclub.co.uk

Havana
42 Blackfriars Street, Manchester M3 2EQ
Telephone: 0161 832 8900

Outdoor Activity Centres
Alternative Adventure and Outdoor Activities
Service
Seddons Farm House, Newington Drive
Bury BL8 2EG
Telephone: 0161 764 3612
Web: www.altadv.co.uk
Activities: abseiling, Canadian canoeing, caving,
climbing, gorge walking, kayaking, sea-cliff
traversing

Pro Adventure
23 Castle Street, Llangollen LL20 8NY
Telephone: 01978 861912
Web: www.adventureholiday.com
Activities: abseiling, canoeing, canyoning, gorge
walking, kayaking, mountain biking, rock
climbing, white-water rafting

A6 Clay Target Centre
Reeves House Farm, Fourgates
Westhoughton, Bolton BL5 3LY
Telephone: 01942 843578
Web: www.a6ctc.co.uk
Activities: clay pigeon shooting

Paintball
Dukinfield Paintball
New Mill, Park Road, Dukinfield SK16 5LX
Telephone: 0161 214 9918

Scuba Diving
Subaqua1
68 Rochdale Road, Middleton M24 2PU
Telephone: 0161 654 6768
Web: www.subaqua-1.co.uk

Skiing & Snowboarding
Runcorn Ski and Snowboard Centre
Town Park, Palace Fields, Runcorn WA7 2PS
Telephone: 01928 701965
Web: www.runcornskicentre.co.uk

Table-side Dancing Clubs
Fantasy Bar
140 Deansgate, Manchester M3 2RP
Telephone: 0161 835 1973

Longlegs
46 George Street, Manchester M1 4HF
Telephone: 0161 237 3977

Tenpin Bowling
Megabowl
White City Retail Park, Chester Road
Old Trafford, Manchester M16 0RP
Telephone: 0161 876 5084
Web: www.megabowl.co.uk

The Dogs
Belle Vue Greyhound Stadium
Kirkmanshulme Lane, Gorton M18 7BA
Telephone: 0870 840 7557
Web: www.bellevuestadium.co.uk

Watersports
Trafford Watersports Centre
Sale Water Park, Rifle Road, Sale M33 2LX
Telephone: 0161 962 0118
Web: www.thedeckersgroup.com

Salford Watersports Centre
Salford Quays, Manchester M5 2SQ
Telephone: 0161 877 7252
Web: www.salford.gov.uk/watersports

NEWCASTLE-UPON-TYNE

Tourist Information Centre
132 Grainger Street
Newcastle-upon-Tyne NE1 5AF
Telephone: 0191 277 8000
Email: tourist.info@newcastle.gov.uk
Web: www.newcastle.gov.uk or www.tyne-online.com

Casinos
Grosvenor Casino
100 St James Boulevard
Newcastle-Upon-Tyne NE1 4BN
Telephone: 0191 260 3303
Web: www.rank.com

Comedy Clubs
The Hyena
Leazes Lane, Newcastle-Upon-Tyne NE1 4PF
Telephone: 0191 232 6030

Cornerhouse Comedy Club
The Cornerhouse Hotel, Heaton
Newcastle-Upon-Tyne NE6 5RP
Telephone: 0191 286 9038
Web: www.funnybonescomedy.co.uk

Flying
Northumbria Helicopters
Newcastle International Airport
Southside, Woolsington NE13 8BT
Telephone: 01661 871433
Web: www.northumbria-helicopters.co.uk

Northumbrian Microlights
1 Bockenfield Cottages, Felton
Morpeth NE65 9QJ
Telephone: 01670 787067
Web: www.northumbrianmicrolights.co.uk

Cleveland Flying School
Teesside Airport, Teesside BL3 1LU
Telephone: 01325 332855

Golf
Newcastle United Golf Club
60 Ponteland Road, Cowgate
Newcastle upon Tyne NE5 3JW
Telephone: 0191 286 4693

Horse Racing
Newcastle Race Course
High Gosforth Park
Newcastle-Upon-Tyne NE3 5HP
Telephone: 0191 236 2020
Web: www.newcastleracecourse.co.uk

Horse Riding
Sinderhope Pony Trekking Centre
High Sinderhope, Allenheads NE47 9SH
Telephone: 01434 685266
Web: www.sinderhopeponytrekking.co.uk

Hot Air Ballooning
Balloons Over The North
Greenacre Lodge, Breadstone, Berkeley GL13 9HF
Telephone: 01453 810018
Web: www.balloonsoverthenorth.co.uk

Karting
Karting North East Indoor
Forge Road, Dunston, Gateshead NE8 2RB
Telephone: 0191 521 4050
Web: www.kartingnortheast.com

Karting North East Outdoor
Warden Law Motorsport Centre
Sunderland SR3 2PR
Telephone: 0191 521 4050
Web: www.kartingnortheast.com

Nightclubs
Sea
Neptune House, Quayside
Newcastle-Upon-Tyne NE1 3RQ
Telephone: 0191 230 1813
Web: www.ultimateleisure.com

Blu Bambu
Grainger Court, Bigg Market
Newcastle-Upon-Tyne NE1 1UW
Telephone: 0191 261 5811
Web: www.ultimateleisure.com

Quay Club
12–20 Dean Street, Newcastle-Upon-Tyne NE1 1PG
Telephone: 0191 261 7771
Web: www.surteeshotel.co.uk

The Lounge
8–10 Neville Street, Newcastle-Upon-Tyne NE1 5EW
Telephone: 0191 261 2211

Tuxedo Princess
Hillgate Quay, Gateshead NE8 2QS
Telephone: 0191 477 8899

Outdoor Activity Centres
Turbo Venture
Pilot House, Corporation Street
Newcastle-Upon-Tyne NE4 5QF
Telephone: 0191 232 5872
Web: www.turboventure.fsnet.co.uk
Activities: abseiling, archery, assault courses, clay
pigeon shooting, flying, military off-road driving,
paintballing, paragliding, quad biking, rope
courses

Premier Leisure
The Pursuits Centre, Slaley Hall, Slaley NE47 0BY
Telephone: 01434 673100
Web: www.premleisure.com
Activities: 4 x 4 off-road Land Rover driving,
archery, canoeing, clay pigeon shooting, climbing,
cross bow and air rifle shooting, mountain biking,
paintballing, quad biking, rally karting

Paintball
National Paintball Games
Opposite Teesside International Airport
Darlington DL2 1LU
Telephone: 0800 072 6969
Web: www.paintballuk.com

Top Gun Paintball
Wayside Cottage, Spawell Road
Ashwell Park, Blaydon NE21 6RS
Telephone: 0191 548 4811
Web: www.topgunpaintballuk.com

Skiing & Snowboarding
Sunderland Ski Centre
Silksworth Sports Complex
Sliksworth, Tyne and Wear SR3 1PD
Telephone: 0191 553 5785

Table-side Dancing Clubs
For Your Eyes Only
25/26 Carliol Square
Newcastle-Upon-Tyne NE1 6UQ
Telephone: 0191 221 2123
Website: www.fyeo.co.uk

Tenpin Bowling
AMF Bowling Newcastle
Westgate Road, Newcastle-Upon-Tyne NE4 8RN
Telephone: 0191 273 0236
Web: www.amfbowling.co.uk

The Dogs
Brough Park Greyhound Stadium
The Fossway, Newcastle-Upon-Tyne NE6 2XJ
Telephone: 0191 265 8011
Web: www.thedogs.co.uk

Watersports
Teesside White Water Course & Kayaking
Tees Barrage Way, Stockton TS18 2QW
Telephone: 01642 678000
Web: www.4seasons.co.uk

Derwent Reservoir Sailing Club
Derwent Reservoir, Blanchland
Consett DH8 9PT
Telephone: 01434 675258
Web: www.derwent-rsc.co.uk

NOTTINGHAM

Tourist Information Centre
Council House, 1–4 Smithy Row
Nottingham NG1 2BY
Telephone: 0115 915 5330
Email: tourist.information@nottinghamcity.gov.uk
Web: www.nottinghamcity.gov.uk

Casinos
Gala Casinos
1–9 Bridlesmithgate, Nottingham NG1 2GR
Telephone: 0115 958 1800
Web: www.galacasinos.co.uk

Gala Casinos
4 Maid Marian Way, Nottingham NG1 6HS
Telephone: 0115 979 9288
Web: www.galacasinos.co.uk

Comedy Clubs

Jongleurs
British Waterways Warehouse
Castle Wharf, Wilford Street, Nottingham NG2 7EH
Telephone: 0870 240 2482
Web: www.jongleurs.co.uk

Flying

Phoenix Flying School
Netherthorpe Airfield, Nr Worksop S8O 3JQ
Telephone: 01909 481802
Web: www.phoenix-flying.co.uk

Golf

Bulwell Forest Golf Course
Hucknall Road, Nottingham NG6 9LQ
Telephone: 0115 976 3172

Edwalton Municipal Golf Course
Wellin Lane, Edwalton NG12 4AS
Telephone: 0115 923 4775

Horse Racing

Nottingham Racecourse
Colwick Park NG2 4BE
Telephone: 0115 958 0620
Web: www.nottinghamracecourse.co.uk

Horse Riding

College Farm Equestrian Centre
West Markham, Tuxford, Newark NG22 0PN
Telephone: 01777 870886
Web: www.haytoncollegefarm.com

Trent Valley Riding Centre
Occupation Lane, Fiskerton
Southwell NG25 0TR
Telephone: 01636 813588

Hot Air Ballooning

Balloons Over Nottingham
Greenacre Lodge, Breadstone, Berkeley GL13 9HF
Telephone: 01453 810018
Web: www.balloonsovernottingham.co.uk

Karting

Amen Corner Karting
Amen Corner, Rufford, Newark NG22 9DB
Telephone: 01623 822205
Web: www.amencornerkarting.co.uk

Express Leisure Karting
Drove Lane, Coddington, Newark NG24 2RB
Telephone: 01636 673322
Web: www.elk-racing.co.uk

Nightclubs

The Works
The Corner House, Burton Street
Nottingham NG1 4DB
Telephone: 0115 938 8780
Web: www.theworks-nottingham.co.uk

Media
The Elite Building
Queen Street, Nottingham NG1 2BL
Telephone: 0115 910 1101
Web: www.themedianightclub.co.uk

Ocean
Greyfriar Gate, Nottingham NG1 7EF
Telephone: 0115 958 0555
Web: www.oceannightclub.co.uk

The Palais
Lower Parliament Street, Nottingham NG1 3BB
Telephone: 0115 950 1075
Web: www.ukcn.com

Libertys
69–71 Upper Parliament Street
Nottingham NG1 6LD
Telephone: 0115 988 1491
Web: www.ukcn.com

Isis
Redfield Way, Nottingham NG7 2UW
Telephone: 0115 986 3211

Outdoor Activity Centres
Off Limits Corporate Events
Units 2, 3 and 9, 100 Baker Road
Newthorpe NG16 2DP
Telephone: 0870 011 7788
Web: www.stagweekends.co.uk
Activities: 4 x 4 driving, abseiling, archery, argo
cats, artic lorry driving, balloon flights, blindfold
tent pitching, bridge over the river why, bungee
running, clay pigeon shooting, cross bow, f1
simulator, falcolnry, fork lift trucks, gladiator
games, golf simulator, helicopter flights, Honda
pilots, horse trekking, hovercraft, human sheep
herding, human table football, It's a Knockout, JCB
driving, microquads, minefield, paintballing, quad
biking, reverse steer driving, tank driving, target
archery

Buggyland II
The National Watersports Centre
Holme Pierrepont, Adbolton Lane
Nottingham NG12 2LU
Telephone: 0115 921 2584
Web: www.buggyland2.com
Activities: archery, laser clay pigeon shooting, mud
buggies, quad biking

Adrenalin Jungle
Sherwood Forest, Nottingham
Telephone: 01623 883831
Web: www.paintball-jungle.co.uk
Activities: 4 x 4 driving, clay pigeon shooting,
military vehicle driving, off-road karting,
paintballing, pony trekking, quad biking

Paintball
Skirmish Paintball Games
Moorfield Farm, Ollerton Road
Oxton, Southwell NG25 0RE
Telephone: 0115 965 7830
Web: www.skirmish.org

Commando Paintball
Nottingham
Telephone: 0115 984 5500
Web: www.nottinghampaintball.co.uk

Skiing & Snowboarding
The Snowdome
Leisure Island, River Drive, Tamworth B79 7ND
Telephone: 0870 500 0011
Web: www.snowdome.co.uk

Tenpin Bowling
AMF Bowling Nottingham
Barker Gate, Nottingham NG1 1JZ
Telephone: 0115 950 5588
Web: www.amfbowling.co.uk

The Dogs
Nottingham Greyhound Stadium
Colwick Park, Nottingham NG2 4BE
Telephone: 0115 910 3333
Web: www.nottinghamdogs.com

Watersports
National Watersports Centre
Adbolton Lane, Holme Pierrepont
Nottingham NG12 2LU
Telephone: 0115 982 1212
Web: www.nationalsports.co.uk

SHEFFIELD

Tourist Information Centre
1 Tudor Square, Surrey Street, Sheffield S1 2LA
Telephone: 0114 221 1900
Web: www.sheffieldcity.co.uk

Casinos
Grosvenor Casino
Queens Road, Sheffield S2 4DF
Telephone: 0114 275 7433
Web: www.rank.com

Flying
Sheffield Aero Club
Netherthorpe Airfield, Thorpe Salvin
Worksop S80 3JQ
Telephone: 01909 475233
Web: www.sheffair.f9.co.uk

Golf
Beauchief Golf Course
Abbey Lane, Sheffield S8 0DB
Telephone: 0114 236 7274
Web: www.beauchiefgolfcourse.co.uk

Horse Racing
Doncaster Racecourse
Leger Way, Doncaster DN2 6BB
Telephone: 01302 304207
Web: www.doncaster-racecourse.com

Horse Riding
Low Ash Riding Centre, Stubbing Lane
Worrall S35 0AP
Telephone: 0114 234 3577

Hot Air Ballooning
See Balloons Over Nottingham, who also fly over
Sheffield, under Hot Air Ballooning for
Nottingham

Karting
Parkwood Karting
Parkwood Road, Sheffield S3 8AH
Telephone: 0114 279 9666
Web: www.parkwoodkarting.com

Nightclubs
Republic
112 Arundel Street, Sheffield S1 1DJ
Telephone: 0114 276 6777
Web: www.gatecrasher.co.uk

Bed
33 London Road, Sheffield
Telephone: 0114 276 6777
Web: www.gatecrasher.co.uk

Kingdom
1 Burgess Street, Barkers Pool, Sheffield S1 2HF
Telephone: 0114 278 8811
Web: www.kingdom-nightclub.com

Club Wow
Valley Centertainment Park, Broughton Lane
Sheffield S9 2EP
Telephone: 0114 243 5670
Web: www.firstleisure.com

Outdoor Activity Centres
Parson House Outdoor Pursuits Centre
Longshaw, Nr Fox House, Sheffield S11 7TZ
Telephone: 01433 631017
Web: www.parsonhouse.co.uk
Activities: abseiling, canoeing, caving, climbing,
kayaking, orienteering

Demon Wheelers
Unit 1, Clarence Works, 30–36 Burton Road
Sheffield S3 8BX
Telephone: 0114 270 0330
Web: www.demonwheelers.co.uk
Activities: 4 x 4 off-road driving, abseiling, archery,
blindfold driving, bungee run, bouncy boxing,
bouncy castle, canoeing, caving, chuckle buggies,
clay pigeon shooting, climbing, cross bow,
gladiator duel, hovercraft, inflatable obstacle
course, It's a Knockout, laser clay shooting, laser
pistols and rifles, minefield game, mountain
biking, off-road racing buggies, paintballing, quad
biking, reverse steer car, rodeo bull, shooting
gallery, waterfall abseiling

Paintball
Ambush Paintball Games Ltd
244 Providence Road, Walkley Bank
Sheffield S6 5BH
Telephone: 0114 285 2850
Web: www.ambushpaintballgames.co.uk

Skirmish Paintball Games
Aizlewoods Mill, Nursery Street, Sheffield S3 8GG
Telephone: 0114 249 3119
Web: www.skirmish.org

Skiing & Snowboarding
Sheffield Ski Village
Vale Road, Parkwood Springs, Sheffield S3 9SJ
Telephone: 0114 276 9459
Web: www.sheffieldskivillage.co.uk

Table-side Dancing Club
Spearmint Rhino
60 Brown Street, Sheffield S1 2BS
Telephone: 0114 279 8092
Web: www.spearmintrhino.com

Tenpin Bowling
AMF Bowling Sheffield
Sicey Avenue, Firth Park, Sheffield S5 6NF
Telephone: 0114 242 5152
Web: www.amfbowling.co.uk

The Dogs
Sheffield Sport Stadium
Peniston Road, Sheffield S6 2DE
Telephone: 0114 234 3074
Web: www.owlertonstadium.co.uk

Watersports
Sheffield Cable Waterski Centre
Rother Valley Country Park
Mansfield Road, Wales Bar S31 8PE
Telephone: 0114 251 1717
Web: www.sheffieldcablewaterski.com

Rother Valley Watersports
Rother Valley Country Park
Mansfield Road, Wales Bar S26 5PQ
Telephone: 0114 247 1453
Web: www.rothervalley.f9.co.uk

MORE ALTERNATIVE ACTIVITIES

Amusement Parks

Alton Towers
Alton, Staffordshire ST10 4DB
Telephone: 08705 204060
Web: www.altontowers.com

American Adventure
Ilkeston, Derbyshire DE7 5SX
Telephone: 0845 330 2929
Web: www.americanadventure.com

Blackpool Pleasure Beach
Ocean Boulevard, South Promenade
Blackpool FY4 1PL
Telephone: 01253 403223
Web: www.blackpoolpleasurebeach.com

Chessington World of Adventures
Leatherhead Road, Chessington KT9 2NE
Telephone: 0870 444 7777
Web: www.chessington.com

Disneyland Paris
Web: www.disneylandparis.com

Drayton Manor Park
Drayton Manor, Tamworth B78 3TW
Telephone: 01827 287979
Web: www.draytonmanor.co.uk

Thorpe Park
Staines Road, Chertsey, Surrey KT16 8PN
Telephone: 0870 444 4466
Web: www.thorpepark.com

Bungee Jumping

UK Bungee Club (various locations)
122 Leeds Road, Lost House, Wakefield WF3 3LP
Telephone: 07000 286433
Web: www.ukbungee.com

Caving

National Caving Organisation
Web: www.nca.org.uk

Cheddar Caves and Gorge
Cheddar, Somerset BS27 3QF
Telephone: 01934 742343
Web: www.cheddarcaves.co.uk

Driving Experiences

Aintree Racing Drivers School
Three Sisters Race Circuit
Bryn Road, Wigan WN4 8DD
Telephone: 01942 270230
Web: www.racing-school.co.uk

Castle Combe Racing School
Castle Combe Circuit, Chippenham SN14 7EY
Telephone: 01249 782417
Web: www.castlecomberacingschool.co.uk

Thruxton Motorsports Centre
Thruxton Circuit, Andover SP11 8PW
Telephone: 01264 882222
Web: www.thruxtonracing.co.uk

Wild Tracks Offroad Activity Park
Chippenham Road, Kennett, Newmarket CB8 7QJ
Telephone: 01638 751918
Web: www.wildtracksltd.co.uk

Knockhill Racing Circuit
Just by Dunfermline, Fife, Scotland KY12 9TF
Telephone: 01383 723337
Web: www.knockhill.com

Mithral Racing
Goodwood Motor Circuit, Chichester PO18 0PH
Telephone: 01243 528815
Web: www.mithral.co.uk

Silverstone Rally School
Silverstone Park, Silverstone, Northants NN12 8TJ
Telephone: 01327 857413
Web: www.silverstonerally.co.uk

Hang Gliding
The British Hang Gliding and Paragliding
Association Ltd
The Old Schoolroom, Loughborough Road
Leicester LE4 5PJ
Telephone: 0870 870 6490
Web: www.bhpa.co.uk

It's A Knockout
Banzai Events
Stratton Court Barn, Pool Farm
Stratton Audley, Bicester OX27 9RJ
Telephone: 01869 278199
Web: www.banzaievents.com
Activities: archery, argo cat, blind driving, clay
shooting, croquet, falconry, helicopters, Honda
pilot racing buggies, hovercraft, It's a Knockout,
karting, kites, power turn rally driving, quad
biking, reverse steering, rodeo bull, sheepdogs,
shooting

Outdoor Concerts & Theatre
Burghley House
Stamford, PE9 3JY
Telephone: 01780 752451
Web: www.burghley.co.uk

Blenheim Palace
Woodstock, Oxfordshire OX20 1PX
Telephone: 01993 811325
Web: www.blenheimpalace.com

Leeds Castle
Maidstone, Kent ME17 1PL
Telephone: 01622 765400
Web: www.leeds-castle.com

Ragley Hall
Alcester, Warwickshire B49 5NJ
Telephone: 01789 762090
Web: www.ragleyhall.com

Kenwood House
The Iveagh Bequest, Kenwood
Hampstead Lane, London NW3 7JR
Telephone: 020 8348 1286
Web: www.english-heritage.org.uk

The Open Air Theatre
The Iron Works, Inner Circle, Regent's Park
London NW1 4NR
Telephone: 020 7486 2431
Web: www.open-air-theatre.org.uk

Minack Theatre and Visitor Centre
Porthcurno, Penzance, Cornwall TR19 6JU
Telephone: 01736 810181
Web: www.minack.com

Ropes Courses
Adventure Rope Co
Fern Hollow, Ruyton, Shrewsbury SY4 1JT
Telephone: 01939 261122
Web: www.adventurerope.co.uk

High Ropes Adventure
Linwood Warren, Legsby Road
Market Rasen, Lincolnshire LN8 3DZ
Telephone: 01526 354182
Web: www.highropesadventure.com

Sailing
Formula 1 Sailing
Haslar Marina, Haslar Road, Gosport PO12 1NU
Telephone: 02392 522388
Web: www.formula1sailing.com

Ahoy! Scotland
63 High Street, East Linton, East Lothian EH40 3BQ
Telephone: 07808 634956
Web: www.ahoy-scotland.co.uk

Yacht Charter
Greencroft, Manchester Road, Sway SO49 6AS
Telephone: 01590 681390
Web: www.yachtcharteruk.com

Surfing
National Surfing Centre
Newquay, Cornwall
Telephone: 01736 360250
Web: www.nationalsurfingcentre.com

Gower Surfing
6 Slade Road, Newton, Swansea SA3 4UE
Telephone: 01792 360370
Web: www.gowersurfing.com

Welsh Surfing Federation Surf School
Llangennith, Swansea SA3 1HU
Telephone: 01792 386426
Web: www.wsfsurfschool.co.uk

Survival Weekends
Survival School
Northwood, Poltimore, Exeter EX4 0AR
Telephone: 01392 460312
Web: www.survivalschool.co.uk

UK Survival School
Seymour House, 24 East Street, Hereford HR1 2LU
Telephone: 01432 376751
Web: www.uksurvivalschool.co.uk

White-Water Rafting
The English White-Water Rafting Committee
c/o Current Trends, Adbolton Lane
Nottingham NG2 5AS
Telephone: 0115 981 8844
Web: www.currenttrends.co.uk

Index